COLONIAL CRAFTS FOR YOU TO MAKE

by Janet and Alex D'Amato

JULIAN MESSNER   NEW YORK

CONTENTS

Messner Books by Janet and Alex D'Amato

COLONIAL CRAFTS FOR YOU TO MAKE

AFRICAN CRAFTS FOR YOU TO MAKE

AFRICAN ANIMALS THROUGH AFRICAN EYES

Published by Julian Messner, a Division of Simon & Schuster, Inc.
1 West 39 Street, New York, N.Y. 10018. All rights reserved.

Copyright © 1975 by Janet and Alex D'Amato

Printed in the United States of America

Library of Congress Cataloging in Publication Data
D'Amato, Janet
Colonial crafts for you to make.
SUMMARY: Introduces various crafts that flourished
during the colonial era and gives instructions for
making replicas of many representative items.
1. Handicraft—Juvenile literature. 2. Handicraft—
United States—Juvenile literature. 3. United States—
Social life and customs—Colonial Period, ca. 1600-1775—
Juvenile literature. [1. Handicraft. 2. United States
—Social life and customs—Colonial period, ca. 1600-
1775] I. D'Amato, Alex, joint author. II. Title.
TT23.D36   745.5/0973   74-19005
ISBN 0-671-32705-4
ISBN 0-671-32706-2 (pb. bdg.)

INTRODUCTION

Daily life was busy and productive in most homes in the thirteen colonies along the Eastern seacoast. By 1750, there were some wealthy families. But most families had little money, and many daily necessities had to be made in the home.

When there was too much to be done, and not enough time or people to do it all, a large family was an asset. Usually each family had eight or ten children—sometimes more. Boys and girls as young as five helped with cleaning, cooking, and other household tasks. Many of them knew how to knit, sew, and weave.

By the time a girl was thirteen, she was able to do as much work as her mother. Boys not only helped inside, they also had outdoor chores.

In small towns and rural areas, most families farmed the land they owned, growing enough food for themselves and fodder for their horse, cow and chickens. Daily tasks for children as well as parents included milking the cow, gathering eggs, and churning the butter. Spring and fall seasons brought much extra work. In spring and summer the garden had to be planted and hoed. In the fall, crops had to be harvested, preserves put up, candles and soap made.

The wealthier families usually lived in the cities. Rugs, wallpaper, furniture, and curios imported from Europe and the Orient made their homes elegant and colorful. The average colonial family could not afford these imports. But, using their own talents and ingenuity, they tried to make their simple homes a little more attractive.

By the middle of the eighteenth century, American craftsmen were making furniture, silver, clocks, and other items that were as good as the imported items. Although most craftsmen used established English designs, they also added their own ideas to

Spring—Planting

Autumn—Harvesting

Summer—Haying

Winter—Preparing flax, cutting logs

what they made. There was intense pride in goods made in the colonies.

Most skilled craftsmen—carpenters, silversmiths, ironworkers, and pottery makers—had their own shops, often employing several people. Young boys were apprenticed to craftsmen to learn needed skills.

While craftsmen created products in shops, itinerant tradesmen such as the shoemaker, weaver, painter and tinsmith traveled through towns and rural areas, carrying their tools in wagons. Much of their pay was farm produce and lodging. These traveling men were a welcome help to get special jobs done.

The crafts and homemade products of a small New England colonial home, just before the revolution, is the topic of this book. The items made either by the householder or the itinerant tradesman are now called folk crafts.

GENERAL INSTRUCTIONS AND MATERIALS

Before starting a project, read the instructions carefully. Then make notes about materials and tools that you will need. Gather together whatever materials you can from around the house, and buy only the few other things you will need.

For some projects, you will be using paint, glue, or stain. So wear a smock to protect your clothes and lay newspapers over your working table. Knives and other tools should always be used carefully. When working with them or with a flame, ask an adult to help. Materials needed will depend on which projects you choose to do.

Cardboard:

For corrugated cardboard, use the side of a supermarket carton. Before cutting the shape needed, draw an outline of the area to be cut. To prevent marking up the tabletop, lay the cardboard on a piece of scrap cardboard. Place a metal-edged ruler along the drawn line and hold firmly. Cut along the edge with a mat knife, being *very* careful of fingers. It is not necessary to press so hard that the knife cuts all the way through the first time. It is better to cut through by going over the line several times, pressing gently. When a lighter weight card is needed, use any discard such as cereal box, pad back, packing for clothes or buy poster board.

Wood:

Balsa wood, used for most models, is available in craft, art, and hobby stores. It can be cut with a coping saw or mat knife. Dowels (round wooden pieces) are available in craft and hardware stores, as well as at lumberyards. Paint stirrers, obtainable from paint or hardware stores, and ice-cream sticks (craftsticks), available in craft stores, are usually made of thin wood and are useful for crafts.

Plastic:

For some projects, rigid plastic discards such as bottle caps or picnic forks are called for. To make holes in this material, heat the tip of an awl in a low flame for a few seconds. When the tip is hot, you will be able to push the awl through the plastic, forming a hole.

Clay and Papier-Mâché:

For shaping small objects, use clay or papier-mâché. Prepared papier-mâché (Celluclay) can be purchased in art or hobby stores, follow directions on the package. Toy, craft, or art stores carry clay (such as "Play-Doh") which will harden in air.

To make a homemade clay, mix together in a pot; ¼ cup EACH of salt, baking soda, and cornstarch. Add ¼ cup cold water. Mix until dry ingredients dissolve. Cook over a low flame, stirring constantly until very thick. Cool; then knead. Soak pot immediately in water and wash. Store clay in a plastic bag in refrigerator; then, when clay is needed, take it out, shape it, and allow it to dry. When hard, clay can be painted.

Glues:

When glue is called for, a white glue (such as Elmer's) can be used, unless another kind is specified. For fabric, use Sobo. To join metals or other hard surfaces, household cement (such as Duco) should be used. These glues are available in most stores, variety, hardware, and craft shops.

If a thick area of glue is needed, or if it is necessary to stick uneven surfaces together, use an epoxy putty such as PC-7. Available in hardware stores, it comes in cans or sticks and has to be mixed; follow package instructions.

Paints and Finishes:

Acrylic paints are excellent for most purposes. They can be thinned and cleaned up with water but are waterproof when dry.

You can also use watercolor (poster) paints or spray paint. Hobby, art, and some variety stores carry acrylic tubes and other paints.

When using spray paint, follow directions on the can. Do the spraying out-of-doors if possible. Place the object to be sprayed in a large cardboard box, and set the box on newspapers to protect surrounding surfaces.

Note: Always allow glue and paint to dry throughly before going on to the next step of the project.

For a finishing coat, use varnish from hardware store or one of the new clear plastic finishes such as Krylon, available in art or hardware stores.

To get an antique effect: after painting an object, let it dry. Then give it a coat of dark brown stain (available at hardware or paint stores). Wipe off the stain before it dries, and it will leave a grained effect.

Tools:

Pictured below are a few basic and inexpensive tools. Depending on the projects you choose to make, only certain tools will be needed. You might have some of these tools around the house. If not, they can be bought in hardware, art, or variety stores.

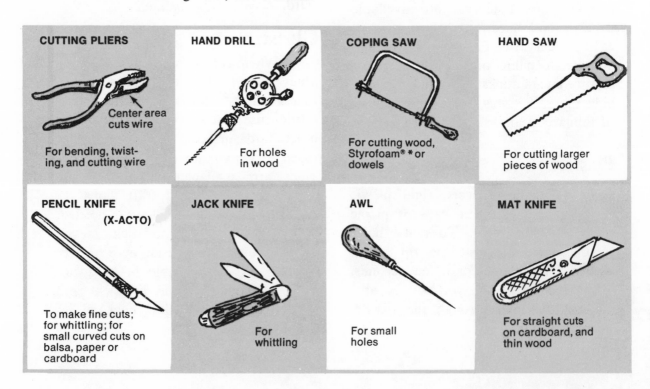

CUTTING PLIERS
Center area cuts wire
For bending, twisting, and cutting wire

HAND DRILL
For holes in wood

COPING SAW
For cutting wood, Styrofoam® * or dowels

HAND SAW
For cutting larger pieces of wood

PENCIL KNIFE (X-ACTO)
To make fine cuts; for whittling; for small curved cuts on balsa, paper or cardboard

JACK KNIFE
For whittling

AWL
For small holes

MAT KNIFE
For straight cuts on cardboard, and thin wood

Trademark of The Dow Chemical Company

Patterns:

To trace patterns from this book, use a lightweight typing paper or use tracing paper (available in art stores). If only half the pattern is given, trace (Fig. 1), then fold the paper in the middle as indicated. Trace other side on the paper (Fig. 2). Open for complete pattern (Fig. 3).

Fig. 1	Fig. 2	Fig. 3
Place on fold	Fold	Open

Some patterns will need to be enlarged. On a sheet of paper, draw the same number of squares as shown in the book, but make them larger. For example, the book will show ½″ squares with instructions to enlarge– ½″=1″. Draw 1″ squares on your paper. Then draw the outline of the object on the larger squares, counting corresponding squares (Fig. 4), and drawing the same lines as in the smaller squares. This makes it easy to get proper proportions on the enlarged pattern.

Fig. 4

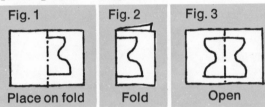

Pattern as it appears in the book (usually shows ½″ squares)

You draw larger squares (usually 1″) and draw on enlarged design

Sewing:

Materials needed for sewing projects include straight pins, thread, a needle, thimble, scissors, and fabric. Needles are sold in packages. For sewing, use size 7/9 sharps or embroidery needles which have larger eyes, making them easier to thread.

To sew by hand, cut a piece of thread about 12″ long. Push one end of the thread through the eye of the needle. Tie a knot in the end of the thread. Put the thimble on your finger as shown in Fig. 1.

Fig. 1

Needle

Thimble

To make a running stitch (basting), push needle into fabric with the thimble. Bring needle tip out again at point about ¼″ away (Fig. 2), and pull up thread. Push needle

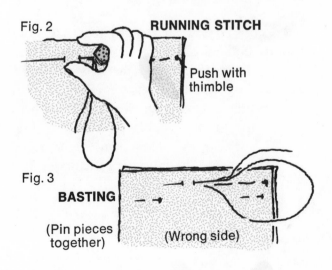

Fig. 2 · RUNNING STITCH

Push with thimble

Fig. 3

BASTING

(Pin pieces together)

(Wrong side)

into fabric again about ¼″ away and repeat (Fig. 3).

To make a seam (such as attaching patchwork pieces), make stitches smaller than basting (Fig. 4). When the stitches are small and close together, the seam will be stronger.

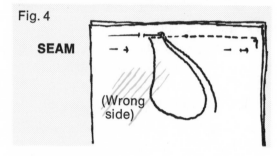

Fig. 4

SEAM

(Wrong side)

For gathering, sew the same as basting, only pull on the thread until it gathers up the fabric (Fig. 5).

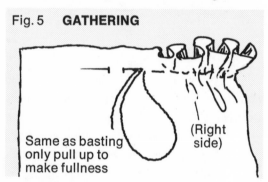

Fig. 5 GATHERING

Same as basting only pull up to make fullness

(Right side)

To sew two edges together, fold in both edges ¼″. Sew through back to front (Fig. 6). A hem is made by folding fabric as shown (Fig. 7). Pin in place. Take a small stitch from hem fabric to fabric below folded edge (Fig. 7); repeat. A rolled hem is the same except that the fabric is rolled over ¼″ or less (Fig. 8).

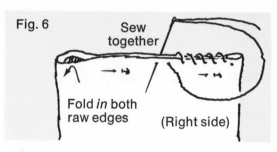

Fig. 6

Sew together

Fold *in* both raw edges

(Right side)

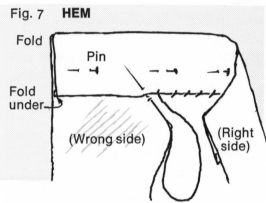

Fig. 7 HEM

Fold

Pin

Fold under

(Wrong side)

(Right side)

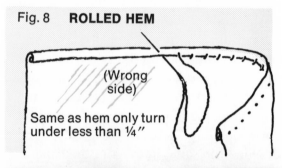

Fig. 8 ROLLED HEM

(Wrong side)

Same as hem only turn under less than ¼″

A colonial child of five could sew a fine seam

A TYPICAL NEW ENGLAND COLONIAL HOME

Wood, plentiful along the East coast, was made into homes with a stone or brick fireplace. The making of brick from native materials was one of the first and most vital industries started in the colonies. By the eighteenth century, towns and cities such as Boston, New York, and Philadelphia had developed along the East coast. Here buildings and homes were often brick structures with many rooms.

As colonists came from Europe, they often built houses here that were similar to the homes they had left. Dutch settlers in New York made brick houses in a style similar to the one used in their homeland. In Pennsylvania, German and Swedish colonists often built homes and barns of stone that had been cleared from the land. Most of the population of the Southern colonies lived on plantations. A large house was surrounded by smaller homes and workshops for servants, farmhands, and such craftsmen as a carpenter, a blacksmith and brickmakers.

An average family's home in the New England of 1750 was a wooden structure built around a fireplace. A man could build this house himself with the help of his sons and neighbors. As he grew richer, he added rooms.

The main room of the house was dominated by a huge brick or stone fireplace. All family activity took place in this room. It served as kitchen, workroom, living room, dining room, and (for some of the family) bedroom.

Pennsylvania House

New England House

Dutch Type House in New York

Southern Plantation

Above, in the peak of the roof, there was a loft or attic where some of the children slept. In back of the fireplace was a pantry or cold-storage area, and to one side there was a small bedroom for the parents. Around the house were small outbuildings for livestock and tools. There was also the "outhouse" (no house had a bathroom in those days).

In summer as well as winter, a fire was always kept burning in the great fireplace. Used for cooking, heating water, and light at night, it was also the only source of heat for the house during bitter New England winters. A new fire was difficult to start since matches did not exist. So if the fire accidentally went out, a child was sent to a neighbor's house with a fire scoop to get a glowing ember.

For cooking, pots were hung from an iron crane embedded into one side of the fireplace. An oven was built either in the back or into one side of the fireplace. Coals from the fire were piled in the oven to heat it. When the oven was hot enough, the embers were removed. Something was almost always baking there: bread, pudding, beans.

Below is a sketch of a typical main room with fireplace. On the following pages are instructions for making a miniature of this room and its furnishings, scaled one inch to equal one foot of actual size. You may add as much furniture and as many small utensils as you like. To get ideas, look at pictures of colonial rooms in library books or visit museum restorations.

A typical colonial room

A neighbor's child (with firescoop) asks for glowing coals to restart a fire.

Model of Room with Fireplace

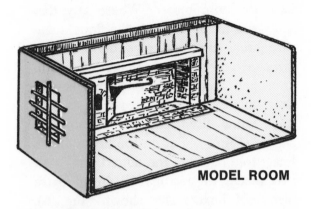

MODEL ROOM

Materials Needed: Start with two clean corrugated boxes; one at least 18″ wide, the other large enough to cut the size shown in Fig. 1. For paneling, use lightweight cardboard, for the crane you will need a square aluminum foil container (from a TV dinner); for bricks use the lids of two egg cartons. For the mantel cut a 10½″ long piece of ½″ x ½″ balsa wood. You will also need paper to trace patterns and black, white, red and brown paint (acrylic is best). Woodgrain areas can be painted brown or cover these areas with adhesive-backed vinyl that looks like woodgrain (¼ yard). Glue, masking tape (available in hardware stores), a paint brush, ruler, scissors, and a mat knife are also needed.

From corrugated boxes cut the two sections. Section one, cut the dimensions shown in Fig. 1. And section two; 16½″ wide by 8″ high, by 9″ deep, as shown in Fig. 2. The fireplace

wall should be a straight piece of corrugated with no seams. If the proper-sized boxes cannot be found, cut sides and floors from separate pieces of corrugated and tape the pieces together to make the room.

Draw a window on section two, dimensions shown (Fig. 2). Cut out. Slide section two into section one, leaving 2″ space at back (Fig. 3). This space (Fig. 4) will be needed later for making the fireplace. Trace through cut window opening, drawing area onto section one.

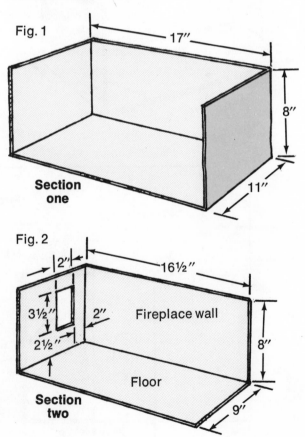

Fig. 1

17″

8″

11″

Section one

Fig. 2

2″

16½″

3½″

2″

Fireplace wall

2½″

8″

Floor

9″

Section two

11

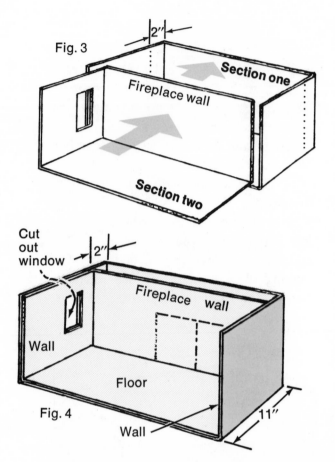

Fig. 3

2″

Section one

Fireplace wall

Section two

Cut out window

2″

Fireplace wall

Wall

Floor

Fig. 4

Wall

11″

Slide sections apart. Cut window out of section one. Tape together any flaps or loose pieces. Where any flap shows on inside walls or the floor, measure area, cut, and glue on an extra piece of corrugated to make a smooth, unbroken area. No flap seams should show inside the room (see Fig. 4).

Draw fireplace and opening as shown (Fig. 5). Cut on the heavy black lines; fold back on the dotted lines. Cut two pieces of corrugated, (from extra pieces of boxes) size shown (Fig. 6). Place these pieces at top and bottom of folded-in fireplace sides; tape in place (Fig. 7). Slide section two back into place. The wall of section one now forms the back of the fireplace. Mark an area 1″ x 10″ on the floor in front of the fireplace. This is the hearth.

Mix black and white paint to make grey. Paint light grey, the fireplace below the mantle area (see Fig. 5,

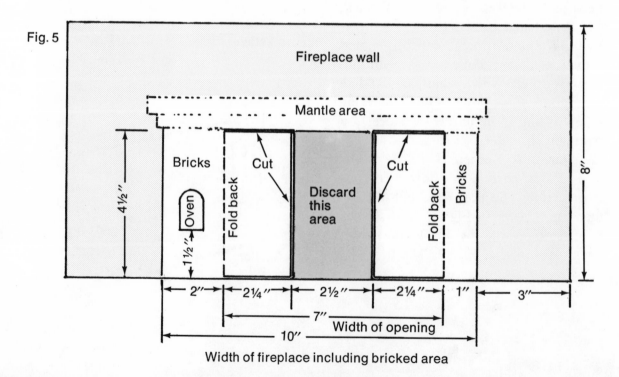

Fig. 5

Fireplace wall

Mantle area

Bricks

Cut

Oven

Fold back

Discard this area

Cut

Fold back

Bricks

4½″

1½″

8″

2″   2¼″   2½″   2¼″   1″   3″

7″

Width of opening

10″

Width of fireplace including bricked area

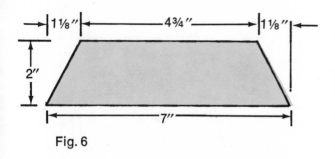

→| 1⅛″ |← ← 4¾″ → →| 1⅛″ |←

2″

← 7″ →

Fig. 6

brick area), and paint the inside and back of the fireplace a dark grey. Paint the top inside of the fireplace black. Paint the hearth light grey (see Fig. 8).

For bricks, cut off the flat top part of two egg cartons. Paint one a brownish red, the other a blackish red. When dry, mark off areas on the wrong side (Fig. 9) and cut as many bricks as possible. Hold bunches of cut bricks, and paint the edges (Fig. 10) to match fronts. Allow to dry.

Trace oven shape (Fig. 11) on a piece of paper, and paint on brick shapes to appear as though you are looking inside the oven. Cut out and glue to left side of fireplace about 1½″ up from floor (see Fig. 5).

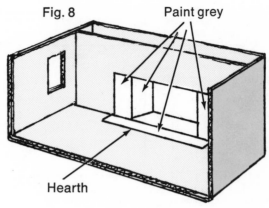

Fig. 8

Paint grey

Hearth

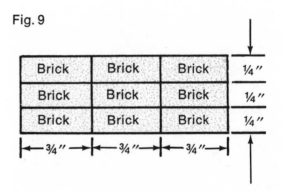

Fig. 9

Brick	Brick	Brick	¼″
Brick	Brick	Brick	¼″
Brick	Brick	Brick	¼″
← ¾″ →	← ¾″ →	← ¾″ →	

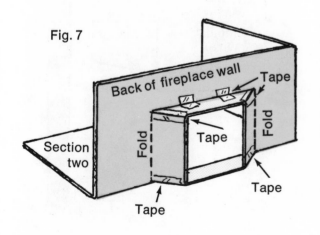

Fig. 7

Back of fireplace wall

Tape

Fold

Tape

Fold

Section two

Tape

Tape

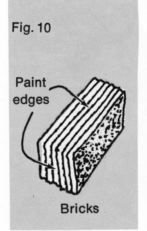

Fig. 10

Paint edges

Bricks

Fig. 11

Oven
Actual size

13

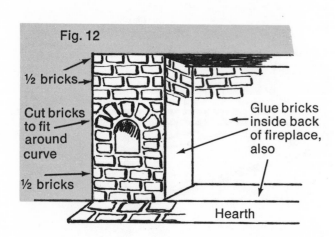

Fig. 12

½ bricks

Cut bricks to fit around curve

½ bricks

Glue bricks inside back of fireplace, also

Hearth

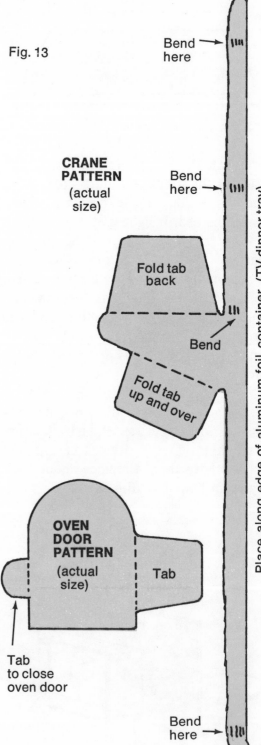

Fig. 13

CRANE PATTERN (actual size)

Bend here

Bend here

Fold tab back

Bend

Fold tab up and over

Place along edge of aluminum foil container (TV dinner tray)

OVEN DOOR PATTERN (actual size)

Tab

Tab to close oven door

Bend here

To attach bricks, work in a small area at a time. Spread glue on the grey surface, and lay bricks in place. Place the darker (blackish red) bricks inside, at the back where the fire would have darkened them. To make the smaller bricks that are needed for corners and edges, cut some bricks in half, paint their edges, and fit them into place. Around the top of the oven, cut bricks at angles to fit (Fig. 12). Cover the hearth with bricks, also. Temporarily separate the two sections again.

Trace shapes (Fig. 13) for oven door and crane on lightweight paper. Place the long edge of pattern of crane along the edge of a foil pan from a TV dinner. Tape in place. With a ball point pen (such as BIC), trace around the drawn crane shape, pressing hard enough to make a dent in the aluminum foil. Trace oven door shape on a flat part of aluminum foil. Remove patterns, and cut shapes of foil along indented lines.

Fold end of crane, up and around as shown (Fig. 14 A and Fig. 14 B). Glue to hold. Paint both pieces black.

With a knife, cut slits through the bricks and the corrugated. For door, make a ¾″ slit at right side of oven and a ⅜″ slit at left side of oven. For crane, cut a 1½″ slit in side of fireplace, with slit ending about 2″ above

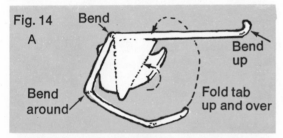

Fig. 14 A

Bend
Bend up
Bend around
Fold tab up and over

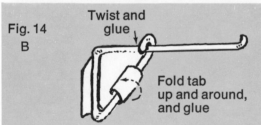

Fig. 14 B

Twist and glue
Fold tab up and around, and glue

floor (Fig. 15). Slip tab of crane into slit, glue, and tape tab in back. Bend tabs of oven door and insert into slits; tape and glue larger oven tab in back. The small tab holds the door closed; yet it can be opened.

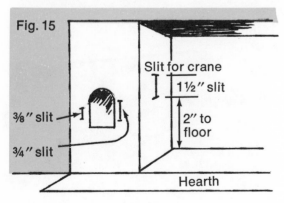

Fig. 15

Slit for crane
1½″ slit
⅜″ slit
2″ to floor
¾″ slit
Hearth

Place two sections of room in position, and glue floor and window wall together.

To make wood paneling for the fireplace wall, cut 8″ long strips of lightweight cardboard: Cut two pieces ¾″ wide, three pieces 1″ wide, and one piece 1¼″ wide. To panel area over fireplace, cut eight pieces 2¼″ long. Four of them should be 1″ wide and the other four 1¼″ wide. Paint panels a brown wood grain color, and their edges dark brown or black. Or, if you like, use the adhesive-backed vinyl which looks like wood grain. Cut vinyl to fit each panel, with ¼″ extra on each side. Peel off backing, stick on, and fold around edges (Fig. 16).

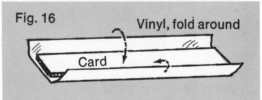

Fig. 16
Vinyl, fold around
Card

For horizontal pieces to go over fireplace, cut two pieces of cardboard. One piece should be 10″ x ½″, and the other should be 10″ x ⅛″. Paint both brown. Glue wider piece over fireplace opening and glue narrow piece on top of that (Fig. 17).

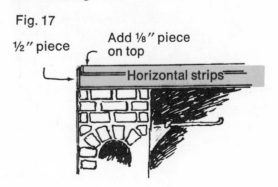

Fig. 17
½″ piece
Add ⅛″ piece on top
Horizontal strips

For the mantle, paint the piece of balsa wood dark brown, or cover it with vinyl. Glue it in place above the horizontal strips (Fig. 18).

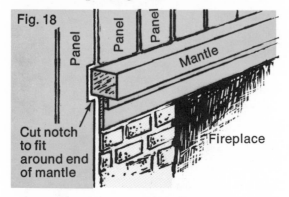

Fig. 18

Panel

Panel

Panel

Mantle

Cut notch to fit around end of mantle

Fireplace

Glue wood grain panels onto the fireplace wall, alternating widths and leaving about 1⁄8″ space between panels. Glue short ones above the mantle over the fireplace. Cut a notch in panel at each end of mantle, if necessary to fit in place (Fig. 18).

Paint the floor brown with black lines to look like floor boards (Fig. 19). Or stick on the vinyl.

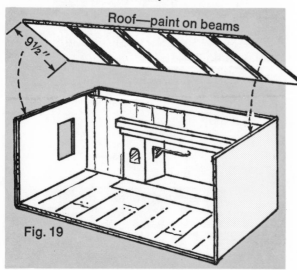

Roof—paint on beams

9½″

Fig. 19

For the roof, cut a piece of corrugated cardboard 9½″ x 18″. Paint white with brown stripes for beams, or stick on brown wood grain strips (Fig. 19). Paint the side walls of the room white.

For window frame, cut ½″ wide strips of thin cardboard, two 3½″ long and two 3″ long. Paint brown. Glue strips around opening (Fig. 20).

To give appearance of windowpanes, cut four 1⁄8″ wide strips of paper or thin cardboard. One strip should be 4″ long, and three strips should be 2½″

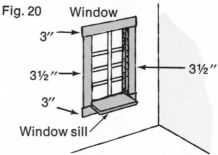

Fig. 20

Window

3″

3½″

3½″

3″

Window sill

long. Glue in position on outside of window opening (Fig. 21). For windowsill, cut a piece of cardboard ¾″ x 2″. Paint brown and glue in position (see Fig. 20).

Place roof piece over room, beams down, to look like ceiling of room (see Fig. 19). Remove roof to arrange furnishings.

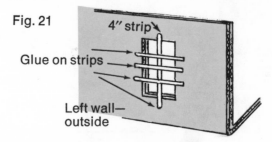

Fig. 21

4″ strip

Glue on strips

Left wall— outside

Colonial Furniture

In early colonial homes, furniture was often homemade. Carpenters and cabinetmakers made good use of American woods to create simple, well-designed furniture. Shown are a few of the popular styles of furniture made by American craftsmen.

Materials Needed: Most of these miniature furniture pieces can be made with 3/16″ balsa wood. When other thicknesses are needed, they are indicated on the pattern. Cardboard can be substituted for thinner pieces. Other "lumber" needed for these projects are ice-cream sticks and the round wooden toothpicks that are natural colored.

Also needed are brown paint or stain, a paint brush, glue, masking tape, and a small hand drill or an awl for making holes, coping saw or knife for cutting wood. After cutting, smooth any rough edges with sandpaper (available in hardware stores). Use the masking tape to hold parts together while glue dries.

With a pencil trace patterns from this book on paper. Turn paper face down on piece of wood. Go over lines to transfer outline to the wood, or place carbon paper over wood, lay on paper and transfer outline to wood.

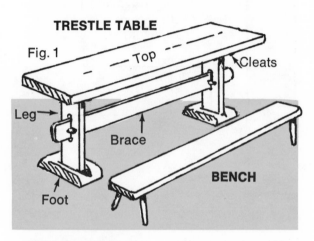

Trestle Table:

On balsa wood draw pieces to size and on thickness indicated in patterns on page 18. Cut out pieces. (Fig. 1.)

To form slot in each leg, drill two holes and then use a knife to cut out the middle (Fig. 2).

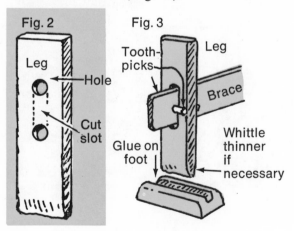

17

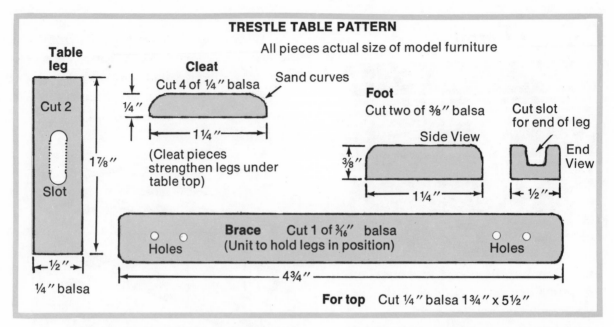

TRESTLE TABLE PATTERN

All pieces actual size of model furniture

Table leg

Cut 2

Slot

1⅞″

½″

¼″ balsa

Cleat

Cut 4 of ¼″ balsa

Sand curves

¼″

1¼″

(Cleat pieces strengthen legs under table top)

Foot

Cut two of ⅜″ balsa

Side View

⅜″

1¼″

Cut slot for end of leg

End View

½″

Brace   Cut 1 of 3⁄16″ balsa

(Unit to hold legs in position)

Holes

Holes

4¾″

For top   Cut ¼″ balsa 1¾″ x 5½″

Make the four holes in brace with an awl. Break a toothpick into four pieces, each about ½″ long. Slide brace into slot (Fig. 3), and insert toothpick pieces in holes on each side to hold brace in position.

Fit legs into slots of foot pieces. If too tight, whittle slightly to make fit. Add glue in slots, and glue in table legs (Fig. 3).

Turn over tabletop and lay flat. Center leg unit on tabletop. Add glue to top of legs; put in place. Glue four small pieces (cleats) on each side of legs (Fig. 4) to strengthen. When glue is dry, turn right side up. With a pencil, press a line in the center of the tabletop to look like boards (see Fig. 1).

Bench:

Cut a 3/16″ thick piece of balsa ¾″ wide x 4½″ long. Using an awl, poke a hole in each corner in the position indicated in Fig. 5. Do not go all the way through the wood. Break toothpicks into pieces 1⅛″ long, add glue to pointed ends, and insert in holes. Turn the bench over, slant legs outward a little bit, and adjust toothpicks so bench sets level (see Fig. 1 on page 17).

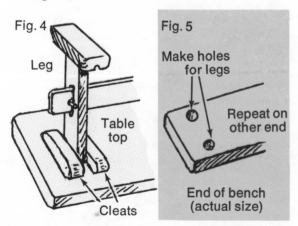

Fig. 4

Leg

Table top

Cleats

Fig. 5

Make holes for legs

Repeat on other end

End of bench (actual size)

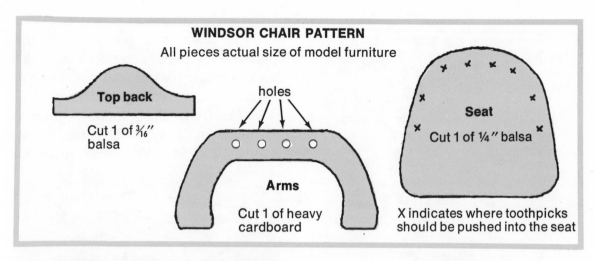

WINDSOR CHAIR PATTERN

All pieces actual size of model furniture

Top back

Cut 1 of ³⁄₁₆″ balsa

holes

Arms

Cut 1 of heavy cardboard

Seat

Cut 1 of ¼″ balsa

X indicates where toothpicks should be pushed into the seat

WINDSOR CHAIR

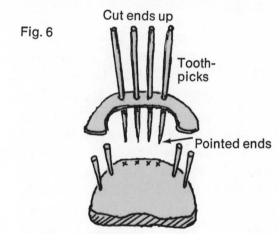

Fig. 6

Cut ends up

Tooth-picks

Pointed ends

Windsor Chair:

Trace patterns above. Cut pieces of the materials indicated. Sand seat and round edges. Use an awl to punch holes that go all the way through the arm piece. Cut four toothpicks 2¼″ long and four others 1″ long. With the awl, make holes in seat, indicated by X's. But do not go all the way through wood.

To make chair back, add glue in holes of arm piece. Slide long tooth-picks through holes; make sure they are even. Add glue to the pointed tips of the four short toothpicks and push them into seat (Fig. 6). Add glue to top of short toothpicks and to the pointed tips of long ones. Push back section into the four holes in back of the seat, with arms resting on short toothpicks. Add extra glue where pieces join. When dry, glue headpiece on top of the four long tooth-picks.

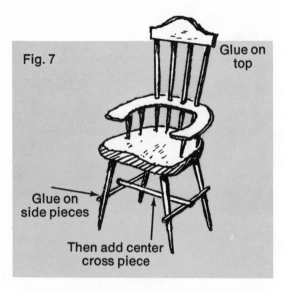

Fig. 7

Glue on top

Glue on side pieces

Then add center cross piece

When top is dry, attach legs. For the legs, break four toothpicks into pieces 1½″ long. Make holes at each corner of the seat, but do not go all the way through the wood. Add glue to tips of picks, push into holes, and set chair down. Angle legs out slightly as shown in Fig. 7, and check that chair sets level. When dry, break a pair of toothpicks into two pieces about 1¼″ long and glue to sides of legs (Fig. 7). Break another toothpick into a piece about 1¾″ for the center cross piece. Glue on, centering on side pieces (Fig. 7).

Cupboard:

On a piece of 3/16″ balsa wood, draw outlines of pieces needed in sizes indicated on pattern on page 22. Trace pattern for sides and mark places where shelves will go. Transfer to wood. Cut sides, shelves, top, front, and back as indicated.

To assemble cupboard (Fig. 8), Glue shelves and top to sides and back. Stick masking tape around unit to hold pieces together while glue dries.

On front piece, indicate a door by indenting lines with a pencil, as shown (Fig. 9). Glue front piece in

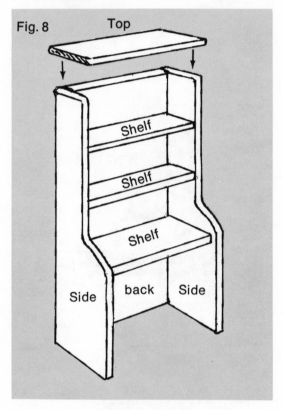

Fig. 8   Top

Shelf

Shelf

Shelf

Side   back   Side

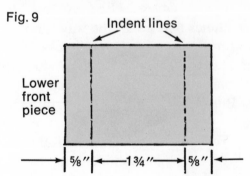

Fig. 9

Indent lines

Lower front piece

5/8″   1¾″   5/8″

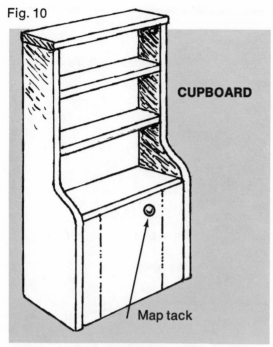

Fig. 10

CUPBOARD

Map tack

place so that top edge of front piece is even with lower shelf (Fig. 10). For doorknob, use a map tack. Add glue to tip, and stick in door.

Allow entire piece to dry completely, and then sand smooth.

Cradle:

Trace patterns on page 22, and cut all pieces indicated. With knife or coping saw cut ice-cream sticks length needed for rockers; whittle ends with knife and sand rockers into curve indicated. For rocker braces, cut another

ice-cream stick in sizes shown (Fig. 11). Glue the brace pieces and rockers to the cradle base (Fig. 12). Allow glue to dry. Glue sides, headboard, and footboard to base piece (Fig. 13), holding in place with masking tape until dry. Glue on top. Sand and smooth all corners. For blanket, cut a piece of fabric 1½″ x 3″ and place inside cradle.

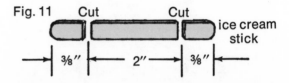

Fig. 11   Cut   Cut   ice cream stick

⊢— ³⁄₈″ —⊣⊢—— 2″ ——⊣⊢— ³⁄₈″ —⊢

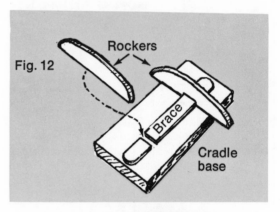

Rockers

Fig. 12

Brace

Cradle base

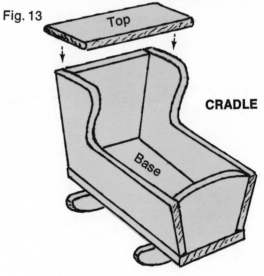

Fig. 13   Top

CRADLE

Base

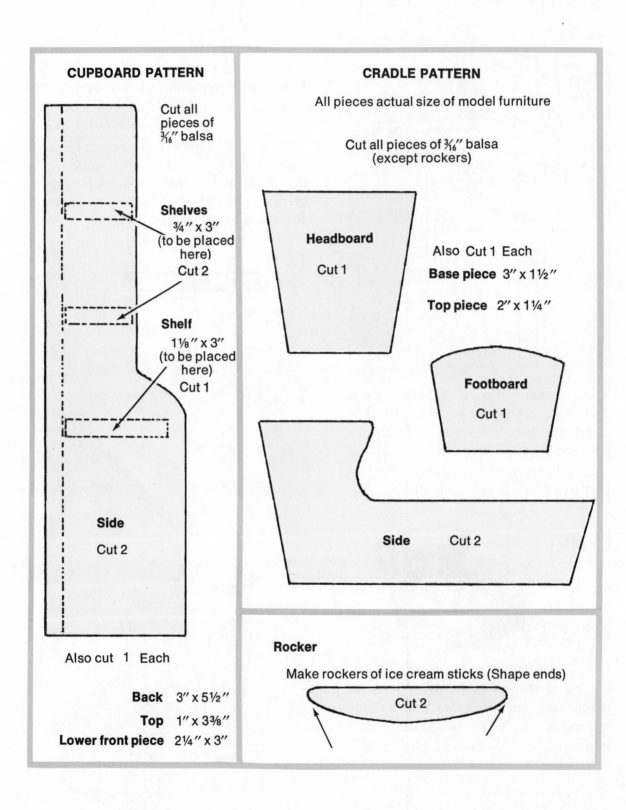

CUPBOARD PATTERN

Cut all pieces of ¾6″ balsa

Shelves
¾″ x 3″
(to be placed here)
Cut 2

Shelf
1⅛″ x 3″
(to be placed here)
Cut 1

Side
Cut 2

Also cut 1 Each

Back 3″ x 5½″
Top 1″ x 3⅜″
Lower front piece 2¼″ x 3″

CRADLE PATTERN

All pieces actual size of model furniture

Cut all pieces of ¾6″ balsa
(except rockers)

Headboard
Cut 1

Also Cut 1 Each
Base piece 3″ x 1½″
Top piece 2″ x 1¼″

Footboard
Cut 1

Side   Cut 2

Rocker

Make rockers of ice cream sticks (Shape ends)

Cut 2

Finishing:

Either stain or paint all furniture in brown tones. Add water to paint making it thin enough so wood grain shows through. (If cardboard is used to make a piece of furniture, it will be necessary to paint that piece).

Other Furniture:

After making the furniture shown, you might want to make other pieces on your own, since the method and sizes (1″ = 1′) have already been shown. For instance, a stool would be the same as the bench; only the top would be a ¾″ round or square piece. Add a piece of felt for a cushion on top (Fig. 14).

A chest would be about the size of the bottom of the cupboard, or a little lower (Fig. 15). Make a small table with four legs the same height as the trestle table (Fig. 16). Make legs of dowels or toothpicks.

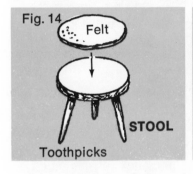

Fig. 14 Felt

STOOL

Toothpicks

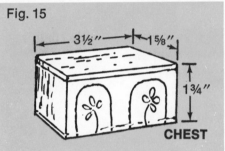

Fig. 15 3½″ 1⅝″ 1¾″

CHEST

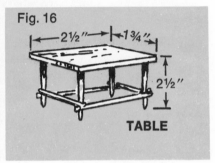

Fig. 16 2½″ 1¾″ 2½″

TABLE

Utensils and Other Household Items

1. Mantle 2. warming pan 3. bellows
4. crane 5. tongs 6. andirons 7. trivet

By the massive fireplace were kept utensils and other practical household items. Large pots, pans and kettles were either hung on the crane or set on trivets in the fireplace. To best use the heat of glowing coals, most cooking utensils had feet. Teakettles and other pots were kept warm by placing on trivets near the coals.

Iron pieces called andirons, supported the logs for the fire. Nearby were tools to tend the fire: shovel, tongs, bellows and a broom. At night the warming pan was filled with glowing embers, then taken to the unheated bedrooms and passed between sheets to warm them.

All sorts of necessary household items accumulated on the mantle: candesticks, lanterns, plates, trays, some pottery jugs, and pitchers. Hanging from the mantle were cooking forks, spoons, and strainers. A variety of drying herbs, corn or peppers also hung from either the mantle or on nearby walls.

The cupboard shelves were filled with dishes, spoons, and knives. Most eating dishes were made of pewter, a metal made by combining tin with other metals. Pewter plates had deep rims because much of the food at the time was in the form of stew. Rich people had china or porcelain dishes, bowls and vases which they imported from Europe and the Orient.

Some of the most beautiful silver items, such as teapots, pitchers, and trays, were made in the colonies by expert silver craftsmen. Most families, (even the poor) had at least one piece, such as a silver candlestick.

Typical items on a cupboard shelf

Materials Needed: To fit the scale of your model room, household utensils and other items will be tiny. The best source of materials will be little things found around the house. Use your imagination to turn discarded bottle caps from shampoo, ketchup, and laundry products into pots. Make homemade clay (see page 5) for other pots and jugs. Clay can also be used to make shapes when you cannot find a properly shaped discard. Black spray paint and glue are also needed for some utensils. Specific materials will be given with each utensil.

Pewter:

You will need aluminum foil trays or pie plates, an old ballpoint pen, one with a point that does not retract (such as a "BIC"), a penny, one button about 3/8" diameter, and household cement.

To make a pewter plate, cut out the flat part of a TV dinner tray or the center of a pie plate. Place a penny on the aluminum foil, and with the ballpoint pen trace around it making a circular dent line on the metal. Cut out circle. Place the shirt button under cutout circle. With the pen, push the aluminum down and around the button, forming a circular dent (Fig. 1). Turn the plate over; remove the button. Shape with pen from right side so that the center of plate is properly indented, like a soup dish (Fig. 2).

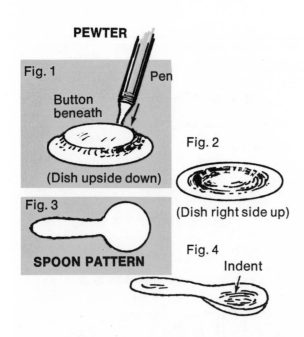

PEWTER

Fig. 1

Pen

Button beneath

(Dish upside down)

Fig. 2

(Dish right side up)

Fig. 3

SPOON PATTERN

Fig. 4

Indent

For spoon, trace shape (Fig. 3) on paper. Lay paper over a piece of aluminum foil. With pen, trace outline through paper, indenting the metal. Remove paper, cut out shape, and place on several thicknesses of old newspaper. Press pen back and forth into bowl of the spoon. This will indent enough to form spoon shape. Indent handle slightly, also (Fig. 4).

For mug, trace shapes in Fig. 5 on paper. Transfer to aluminum and cut out. Curve to make mug shape, and glue handles together. When dry, indent center of handle (Fig. 6). Glue mug to base.

Make several of each pewter piece.

For platter, trace oval shape on paper (Fig. 7). Transfer to aluminum and cut out. Indent slightly along line

shown. Place on table or mantle of model room. If platter does not stand properly on mantle (Fig. 8) glue to the wall above mantle.

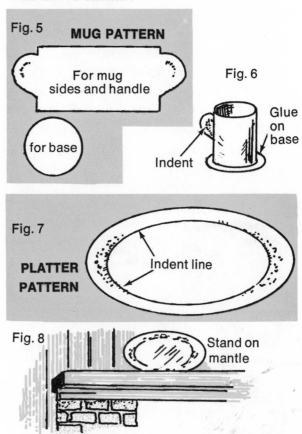

Fig. 5 **MUG PATTERN**

For mug sides and handle

for base

Fig. 6

Glue on base

Indent

Fig. 7

PLATTER PATTERN

Indent line

Fig. 8

Stand on mantle

Pots and Trivet:

You will need clay, papier-mâché, or appropriate-sized bottle caps, as well as straightened paper clips or wire (copper wire bends easily), wire-cutting pliers, epoxy putty, and household cement.

Find discarded caps, or shape clay or papier-mâché into a pot or pan in approximately the size shown (Fig. 1). For handle, make holes with an awl in the clay or papier-mâché while still soft. Cut wire length indicated; shape, insert, and glue into position (Fig. 2). Make feet by cutting ⅜″ off the end of round toothpicks. Insert feet.

If using a metal bottle cap, glue handle inside top edge (Fig. 3). Add a little thickness at bottom with epoxy putty to give more of a rounded look to pot bottom (Fig. 3). For feet, insert toothpicks into putty. Paint black.

that trivet stays level (Fig. 7). Paint trivet (and other iron objects) black.

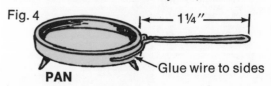

PAN

Fig. 4 — 1¼″ — Glue wire to sides

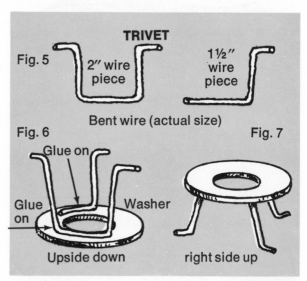

TRIVET

Fig. 5 — 2″ wire piece — 1½″ wire piece

Bent wire (actual size)

Fig. 6 — Glue on / Glue on — Washer — Fig. 7

Upside down — right side up

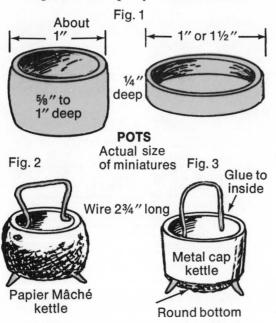

POTS
Actual size of miniatures

Fig. 1
About 1″
⅝″ to 1″ deep
1″ or 1½″
¼″ deep

Fig. 2
Wire 2¾″ long
Papier Mâché kettle

Fig. 3
Glue to inside
Metal cap kettle
Round bottom

Andirons:

For pan, glue toothpick feet to bottom and wire handle to sides (Fig. 4) using household cement.

For trivet, cut and bend paper clip or wire (Fig. 5). Glue both pieces to a 1″ diameter washer (Fig. 6). When glue is dry, turn over and adjust feet so

To make two, these materials are needed: a large-sized paper clip for each andiron, or a piece of heavy wire 6¼″ long, two small beads about ⅛″ diameter. cutting pliers, hammer, and either epoxy glue or household cement.

For lower front section, unfold clip and, with pliers, cut off a 2″ piece. Shape with pliers as shown (Fig. 1).

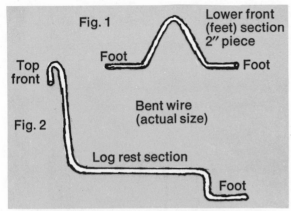

Fig. 1
Lower front (feet) section 2" piece
Foot
Foot
Top front
Fig. 2
Bent wire (actual size)
Log rest section
Foot

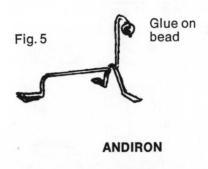

Fig. 5
Glue on bead

ANDIRON

Use remaining piece of clip to make the top front and the log rest section. Bend as shown (Fig. 2).

Lay wire pieces on top of a vise or a flat rock, and hold with pliers. Hit with hammer to flatten a little bit the three wire feet on each andiron (Fig. 3).

Lay front feet section over log rest section (Fig. 4) and glue together. The pliers can hold the pieces while glue sets. Glue a small bead on front tip, if desired (Fig. 5). Paint black.

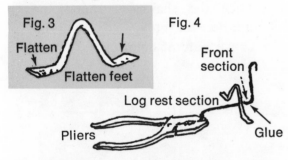

Fig. 3
Flatten
Flatten feet
Fig. 4
Front section
Log rest section
Pliers
Glue

For logs, find some twigs ¼" or less in diameter and break into pieces about 3" long. Set the pair of andirons in fireplace, and lay several twigs across to look like firewood (Fig. 6). Place more logs at the side of the fireplace. Hang pot on the crane in the fireplace.

Fig. 6
Wood

Herbs, Flowers, and Pots:

You will need dried grasses and weeds, small pins (sold in craft stores to attach sequins), papier-mâché or a piece of clay (see page 5). To make clay grey, knead in a little black paint.

Select dried materials that are about the size and shapes shown (Fig. 1). Tie in bunches. Tack to mantle and wall using the sequin pins. Or glue on.

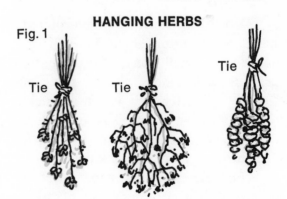

HANGING HERBS
Fig. 1
Tie
Tie
Tie
Tie

CROCKERY

Fig. 2

Actual size

Plate

Crock

Crock

Jug

Jar

WARMING PAN

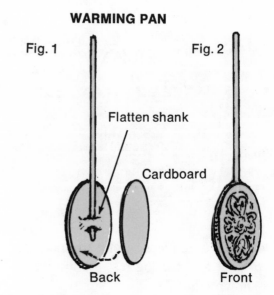

Fig. 1

Fig. 2

Flatten shank

Cardboard

Back

Front

Use drawings (Fig. 2) as a guide to the size and shaping of clay or papier-mâché. Make a flower pot (Fig. 3). While clay or papier-mâché is soft, arrange tiny dried flowers in it. When dry, set on table.

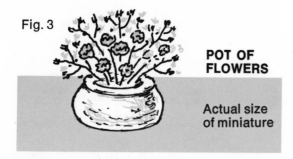

Fig. 3

POT OF FLOWERS

Actual size of miniature

Warming Pan and Broom:

You will need a brass-colored shank metal button about 1″ or 1¼″ diameter, a small piece of cardboard, and, for each handle, a 3½″ piece of stick ⅛″ diameter such as a swab stick, lollipop stick or a dowel. Also needed: a scrap piece of balsa wood, tan thread, glue, brown paint, and a knife.

For the warming pan, select a decorative button. Insert end of stick into shank of the button. So that the stick will hold, flatten shank by pounding it gently with a hammer (Fig. 1). Cut a cardboard circle the same size as the button, and glue to back. Paint cardboard and handle brown (Fig. 2).

For broom, use a sharp knife to shave the balsa wood, moving with the grain, into narrow strips about 1¼″ long. Glue the shavings around the stick, and tie with thread (Fig. 3). Trim ends. Leave natural color.

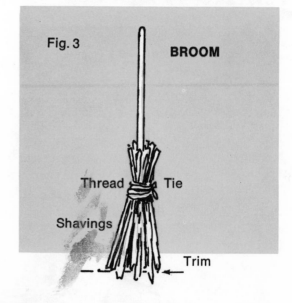

Fig. 3

BROOM

Thread

Tie

Shavings

Trim

Lighting

Candle making

Colonists were up at dawn, busy at their chores. No precious hour of daylight could be wasted. At night, the glow of the fire often provided the only light in the room. There were torches and various types of lamps that burned oil, but they were too smoky and smelly to be used much indoors. Candles were used very sparingly as candle making was a difficult job. Those who could afford to, bought candles and soap in the chandler's shop. Also, traveling chandlers went from house to house making candles.

Candlesticks, chandeliers, and wall sconces of many designs held the candles. On the wall, the candle was usually set in a sconce which had a reflector behind it to increase the light. Lanterns were used as a means of carrying lighted candles around.

Sconce, Candle holders, Lantern

Candle Holders:

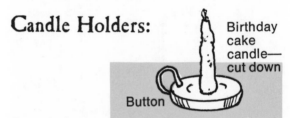
Birthday cake candle— cut down

Button

To complete your miniature room, make some miniature candles and candle holders.

Materials Needed: Silver or brass colored flat buttons (or a tack or a small bottle cap), that are about ½″ in diameter, a ¾″ piece of thin wire and some white birthday candles.

Bend wire into loop. With household cement, glue wire loop to the button, tack, or cap (Fig. 1) To complete, add candle (see next page).

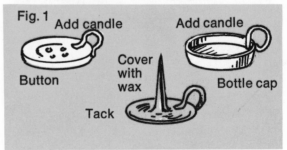
Fig. 1 Add candle   Add candle

Button   Cover with wax   Bottle cap

Tack

Silver Candlestick:

Materials Needed: A small, black or silver, flat-top shank button about ½" in diameter; 2¼" piece of thin wire, five or six silver beads in various sizes and shapes, and one silver sequin.

Slip one end of wire through the shank of the button; twist and glue with

SILVER CANDLESTICK

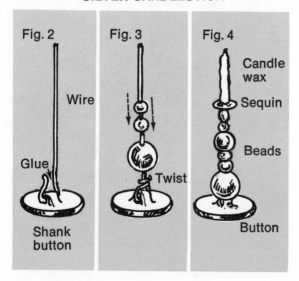

household cement so wire remains vertical (Fig. 2). Add glue to wire, and slide on silver beads (Fig. 3). Add glue to top bead, and slide on the sequin. Add wax to wire (Fig. 4) for candle (see below).

Candles:

With paring knife, whittle a birthday-cake candle to fit size shown (Fig. 5). Glue in place on button or cap. For

the tack or silver candlestick, remove some candle drippings, (while still warm) from a regular candle. Press wax around wire with fingers to form a candle shape (see Fig. 4).

Wall Sconce:

For a pewter look, use a piece of an aluminum foil plate.

Trace pattern (Fig. 6); transfer to piece of aluminum (see Pewter, page 24). Cut out, indent, and shape with ball-point pen.

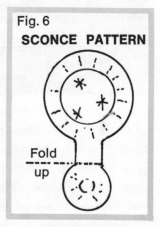

Fold as indicated. Cut birthday candle ½" long. Glue on (Fig. 7). Glue sconce on wall of model room.

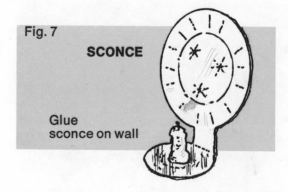

COOKING

Big meals were cooked either directly over the fire or in the oven. Those pots and kettles that hung in the fireplace were made of heavy iron, often weighing as much as forty pounds. Cooking and preparing food was a long process and took most of the day. This was especially so in the fall when the crops were harvested.

Most all foods for the family were grown or raised on their own land and were processed at home. Many methods were used to preserve foods for there was no refrigeration. Foods were smoked, salted, dried, pickled, or made into jams. Usually, a pot of stew was kept simmering over the fire day and night. As long as the stew stayed hot, it wouldn't spoil and the family could eat it all week.

Flour was made of wheat or corn which had to be ground at the grist mill. Then bread was baked at home. Dairy products, such as butter and cheese, were made from milk from the family cow. By the time a child was five-or-six-years old, he spent many hours churning the cream into butter.

Active, busy families had hearty appetites. Meals consisted of meats or game, several vegetables (usually including beans), meat pies, bread, biscuits or cornmeal. To complete the meal there were fruits, cookies and cakes. Some colonial foods were similar to what we eat today; others were odd named dishes such as Flummery, Sillabub, and Hasty Pudding.

Flummery:

Flummery seems to be a general name for a fruit pudding. Old recipes for it vary greatly. Some flummery was thin like soup; other kinds were thicker. Some was simply cooked fruit thickened with cornstarch. Others included a number of ingredients, such as fresh lemons, sugar, milk, and eggs or isinglass (a type of gelatin) for thickening.

Here is a recipe for flummery, using modern ingredients. The packaged gelatin replaces the fresh lemon, sugar, and isinglass.

  Strawberry Flummery
  1 package of lemon-flavored
    gelatin
  1 cup boiling water
  1½ cups milk
  1 package of frozen strawberries,
    thawed

Dissolve gelatin in boiling water. Cool until slightly thickened. Slowly stir in cold milk. Beat for a few seconds with a hand mixer. Add thawed fruit. Pour into serving dishes and chill.

SPINNING, DYEING, AND WEAVING

Every colonial household required many items made of fabric. Bed linens, napkins, and curtains were needed, as was clothing for the entire family. Most fabric was made at home, a long process which often took more than a year.

Linen and wool were the most commonly used fibers. Linen was made from flax which the colonists grew. Only after a hard, tedious process were the stalks ready to be spun into linen threads. The colonists also raised sheep for their wool. In fact, wool was in such demand that sheep were protected by laws and were only used for their wool.

Spinning, a process of twisting short fluffy pieces of flax or wool into thread, was done with a spinning wheel. The large wheel turned the small spindle to which the ends of loose fibers

were attached. As a woman pushed and pulled the fibers, the spindle twisted them. Practice was needed to keep proper tension as the fibers twisted. At a very young age, girls learned to spin. Mothers and grandmothers were never idle, and when friends visited, the spinning wheel hummed as they chatted. Visitors often brought their own spinning wheels with them.

After the spinning was done, the threads were either knitted or woven into cloth. Most colonial homes had a huge loom for weaving large pieces of cloth. Men usually did the weaving as the loom took strength to operate. Some families waited until the traveling weaver arrived. He would stay with the family, weaving fabrics until all the yarns the women had spun were used up. Then he would go on to the next family. Sometimes he carried his own loom. There were also weavers' shops in some towns where homespun thread was woven into cloth. The most common fabric made in colonial times was linsey-woolsey, a combination of linen and wool.

Dyeing:

Natural spun yarns were a dull tan or a grey color. To weave patterns or make colored fabric, it was necessary to dye the yarn. Women gathered various barks, roots, berries, and plants; then they boiled and strained them to make dyes.

Browns, yellows, some reds, and green (from grass) could be made from the local vegetation. Blue came mostly from indigo, a plant grown in the tropics. In 1740, a young South Carolina girl had some indigo plants brought from the island of Barbados in the Caribbean. The indigo grew so well that it became an important product of the colonies. Whenever blue color was desired, a small lump of indigo was added to a dye pot.

To Make Dye: For yellow or brown, just as it was done two hundred years ago, remove enough skins from yellow onions to make about one cup of skins. Boil skins in two cups of water for half an hour. (If there are too many minerals in the water in your area, use rain water to make the dye.) Remove the skins from the dye pot. Add ½ cup vinegar, which will make the dye permanent. Place wet white wool yarn (or a piece of white cotton or wool fabric) in the pot. Simmer over a very low heat until material reaches desired color. It takes about fifteen minutes to make yellow; brown takes about half an hour.

When the color is right, lift the yarn or fabric from pot using a stick or fork. Then lay it on a paper towel to remove excess moisture. Hang to dry.

Weaving: (portable loom)

Not all weaving was done on huge looms. Various small ones were used to weave narrow pieces, and some were portable. Children learned to weave on a type of lap loom. A boy would weave his own suspenders or shoelaces; girls wove ribbons or cords.

Here is a simplified portable loom to make. With it you can weave a narrow strip to use as a belt, strap, or just to hang up as a decoration. The basic piece of the loom, called a heddle, has alternate slots and holes that control lifting of the warp threads.

Materials Needed: For the heddle, use seven plastic picnic forks, masking tape, an awl, two ice-cream sticks, some small thumbtacks, a yarn needle and sturdy thread (buttonhole twist is good). For weaving you will need two colors of a medium-weight yarn.

To make heddle, lay the plastic forks on a piece of masking tape alternately as shown (Fig. 1), leaving about

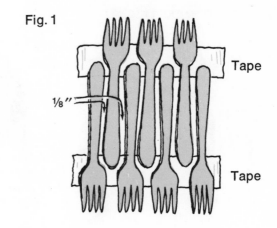
Fig. 1
Tape
⅛"
Tape

⅛" between fork handles. Press on tape to hold. Heat the tip of an awl in a low flame and push the awl through each fork handle, making three rows of holes (Fig. 2).

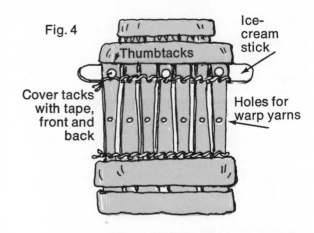

Fig. 4

Thumbtacks

Ice-cream stick

Cover tacks with tape, front and back

Holes for warp yarns

Fig. 2

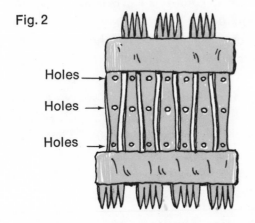

Holes →
Holes →
Holes →

Using a heavy needle threaded with sturdy thread, go in and out of the top row of holes (see A, B, and C of Fig. 3). Repeat across bottom row of holes. To keep stiff, place an ice-cream stick under top row of holes. Push thumbtacks through three holes, pushing in just enough to hold, but not coming out in back. Add more tape front and back to cover thumbtacks and edges of forks (Fig. 4).

Now the heddle is ready to thread. The long pieces that are controlled by the heddle are called "warp." To make a short practice piece that you can use as an armband or a bookmark, cut nineteen pieces of yarn, eight dark and eleven of a light color, each about one yard long. (After you're ready to make an item of specific length, such as a belt, measure the length needed, add at least an extra 18" on each end).

Using yarn needle, thread one strand of yarn through the first hole in heddle. Next, push two yarn strands through slit. Next hole, thread needle with another strand of yarn and go

Fig. 3

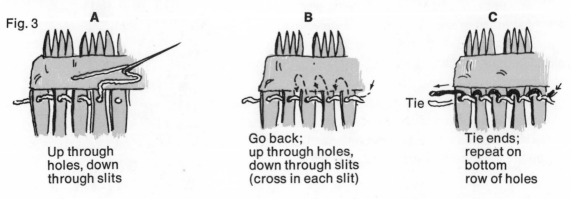

A

Up through holes, down through slits

B

Go back; up through holes, down through slits (cross in each slit)

C

Tie

Tie ends; repeat on bottom row of holes

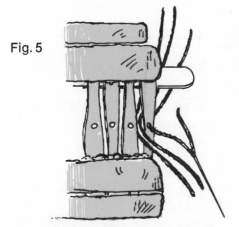

Fig. 5

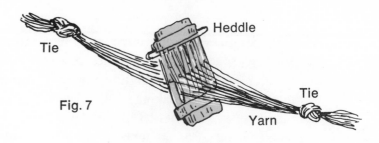

Tie

Heddle

Fig. 7

Tie

Yarn

through hole (Fig. 5). Continue across heddle. To create a pattern, suggested placement for light and dark colors is shown in Fig. 6.

Knot ends of warp together with a loose knot (Fig. 7). Repeat on other end.

Tie one end of the bundle of yarn strands to a chair back, handle, knob, tree, or bedpost. Sit on a chair and tie the other yarn ends to your belt. Move your chair back just far enough to make yarn warp taut. Lift the heddle. All the warp going through the holes should be lifted up (Fig. 8); all the warp in the slits will remain lower. This space (where the weaving yarn will pass through) is called a shed. When the heddle is pushed down, the yarn in the holes should be pulled below the warps that are in the slots; this space formed is the opposite shed. Move heddle up and down until it works.

Fig. 6

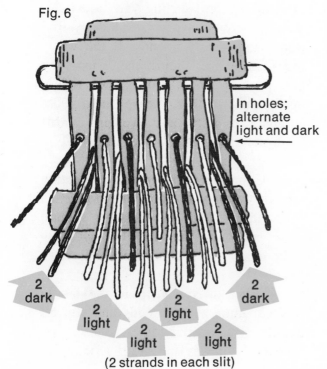

In holes; alternate light and dark

2 dark

2 light

2 light

2 light

2 light

2 dark

(2 strands in each slit)

Fig. 8

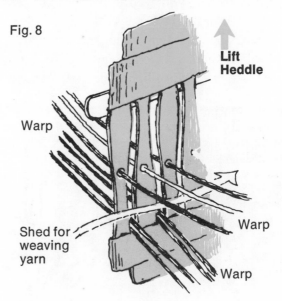

Lift Heddle

Warp

Shed for weaving yarn

Warp

Warp

To begin weaving, warp should be properly spaced. Take another ice-cream stick and weave over and under the alternate warps, making a flat row near the knot at your belt (Fig. 9). This can be removed after an inch or so of fabric is woven.

To weave, cut two pieces of yarn, one dark, one light, each about one yard long. Tie end of dark piece near knot, at your belt. Lift heddle and pass yarn through the shed; lower the heddle and pass yarn back through the opposite shed. Repeat; weaving yarn to left. Change shed, back to right. Change shed, to left again. And so on.

To push yarn down evenly, use a small 6″ ruler or stick. Slide the stick into the shed after putting yarn through, and push down, sliding the newly woven yarn piece against the last row. Make it even, but not too tight. Do this with each row as you weave.

Weave four rows of dark color, then start the light. Tie end on warp, two strands from edge; go out to edge and start weaving light (Fig. 10). Weave three rows of light. Pick up dark thread (it can be left hanging while working other color), and weave four more rows. Then pick up the light and weave three rows, repeating this over and over again.

A pattern should begin to appear. The heddle has been making the weaving go under 1, over 2, under 1, and so on, and the reverse on the next row. If it is not working this way (Fig. 11), check heddle to make sure yarn warp is sliding in the slots as planned and that you are lifting it properly.

Do not pull yarn too tight, or the pattern won't come out right. Try to keep the woven piece the same width throughout. If it gets narrower, you are pulling the weaving yarn too tight. You should weave more loosely—but don't leave loops at ends. If the weaving threads are hiding the warp, you are pushing them down too tightly against each other. Leave them loose enough so warp and weaving yarns form neat squares to make design (Fig. 12).

Continue weaving up. If section already woven is too long to reach over, untie, fold woven strip around your belt, and pin it. New weaving area again is a comfortable distance to work.

When woven strip is the length desired, untie at both ends and slip off heddle. Tie warp ends, as shown, on both ends of weaving (Fig. 13).

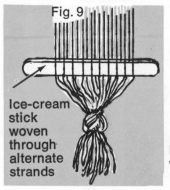

Fig. 9

Ice-cream
stick
woven
through
alternate
strands

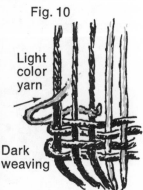

Fig. 10

Light
color
yarn

Dark
weaving

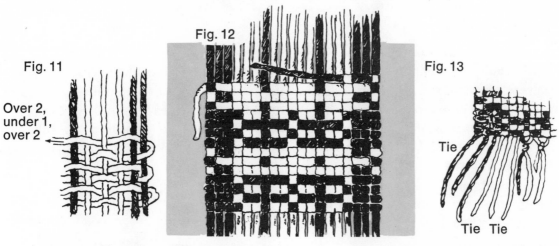

Fig. 11

Over 2, under 1, over 2 →

Fig. 12

Fig. 13

Tie

Tie Tie

Although light and dark arrangement of yarn is suggested, any arrangement can be used so long as colors repeat in sequence. Each arrangement creates a different checked-type pattern.

A lap loom of this type is portable, so the weaving can be tied on anywhere firm, and then untied and put in a box when you're ready to go somewhere else.

If this type of weaving appeals to you, maybe you know someone who does wood working and who could make a sturdy heddle or lap loom of wood by sawing slits and drilling holes. Ten or fifteen holes will make wider weavings. Sand wood smooth, thread the heddle, and weave. Many craft stores carry wooden or plastic heddles.

PATCHWORK AND QUILTING

When you think about the amount of work it took to make a piece of fabric in colonial days, you can understand why no fabric was discarded. Even when clothes or other items began to wear out, patches were added to prolong their use. Every household had a rag bag filled with pieces used to patch and repair fabrics. Sometimes threads were unraveled, dyed again, and rewoven into new pieces.

One of the most common uses for pieces of fabric was in making quilts.

Small odd-shaped pieces were sewn together and decorated with embroidery along the pieced edges. This was the "Crazy Quilt." Small geometric shapes were also sewn together to form squares. The squares, as many as a

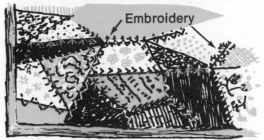

Embroidery

Crazy Quilt

hundred, made a patchwork quilt. Designs were given names, such as those shown below. These are a few of the many possible ways of piecing a square. Often the most colorful thing in a colonial home was the pieced quilt.

A small girl began sewing by stitching together small patchwork pieces. Each stitch had to be tiny and even.

All winter, women and girls worked on their piecing, making the top layer. In the spring and summer, these coverlets were made into quilts. The quilting frame, which was too large to set up in a room filled with family activity, usually was set up outside where the women and girls of the area gathered to help quilt.

Quilting turned the piecework into a warm bedcover. A backing of plain fabric was stretched across the frame. Over this was laid stuffing material. Then the quilted piece was put in place, pinned, and basted together.

Everyone sat around the frame sewing tiny stitches in a predetermined design until the entire area was quilted. Decorative quilting also appeared on other items such as pockets and petticoats.

Quilt a Potholder

Materials Needed: Sturdy cotton fabric (or something similar), a 7″ square piece of patterned fabric for the front, a 8½″ x 12″ piece of plain fabric for the back. For padding, use a 7″ square of any new or used material (wool cloth, terrycloth, or a discarded ironing board cover). Also needed are two wooden coat hangers, a sewing needle, and thread to match patterned fabric.

Select a simple design for patterned fabric, such as a geometric or one large flower (Fig. 1).

Quilting frames have devices that tighten, keeping the fabrics taut at all

Log Cabin

Tail of Ben's Kite

Shoo Fly

Garden of Eden

Fig. 1

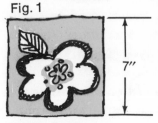

7″

Large flower print

Geometric Print

times and leaving both hands free for sewing. For a small piece such as this, two wooden coat hangers can serve the purpose.

Baste the backing fabric to straight bar of each hanger (Fig. 2). Lay padding piece on the backing fabric (Fig. 3); then place the patterned fabric on top, right side up. Baste the three pieces together. Turn hook of top hanger so it is at right angles to hanger. Hook this hanger to a drawer pull. To make the fabric taut, sit on a chair and hook the other hanger to your belt. Move chair just far enough away to stretch the fabric between hangers (Fig. 4).

Thread needle, and sew in and out making tiny running stitches through all three layers (Fig. 5). Keep one hand underneath to guide needle while other hand stitches on top. For pattern, follow the design on the fabric (Fig. 6). In blank areas, sew some lines or curves as all areas should have a little quilting.

Check the back occasionally to make sure it is as neat as the front. Keep thread knots at the side where they will be covered with binding.

When quilting is complete, remove all basting and take off hangers. Trim under layers even with top layer. Sew a bias binding all around, leaving about 3″ extra at one corner (Fig. 7). Sew down end to make a hanging loop to complete potholder.

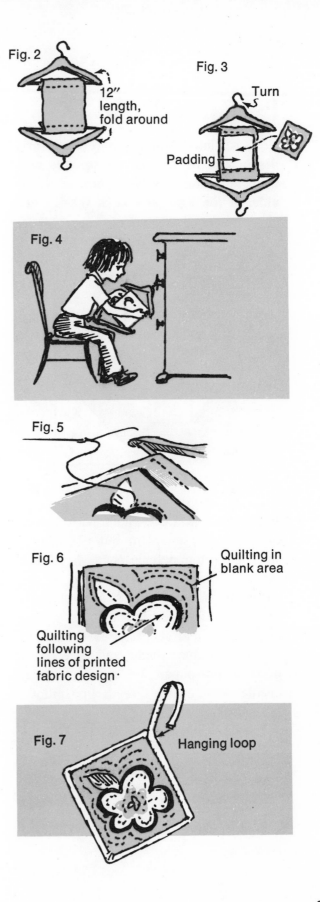

Fig. 2
12″ length, fold around

Fig. 3
Turn
Padding

Fig. 4

Fig. 5

Fig. 6
Quilting in blank area
Quilting following lines of printed fabric design·

Fig. 7
Hanging loop

Patchwork Pillow

An interesting colonial patchwork design can be created of squares and triangles using any color fabrics available. If the light and dark fabrics are cleverly placed (as in Fig. 1), a pattern is created called "Monkey Wrench."

Fig. 1

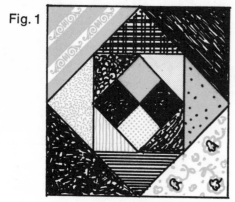

Monkey Wrench

Materials Needed: Start with pieces of fabric that are firm but not heavy, such as cotton percale (bed sheets are made of this material). Select an assortment of solid colors and patterns that go well together, such as prints, polka dots, and stripes. Fabrics should all be the same weight and type. Also needed are paper for patterns, pins, needle, and sewing thread. For pillow, a 20" square of fabric for back and Dacron or shredded foam stuffing will be needed.

For patterns, enlarge the shapes shown (Fig. 2) on graph paper. Make

sure all corners are right angles. Outside line is the cutting line, and the inside line the sewing line. Cut out the paper patterns.

Press materials smooth. Lay the patterns on the fabric with one edge along the grain (direction in which the threads go) of the material.

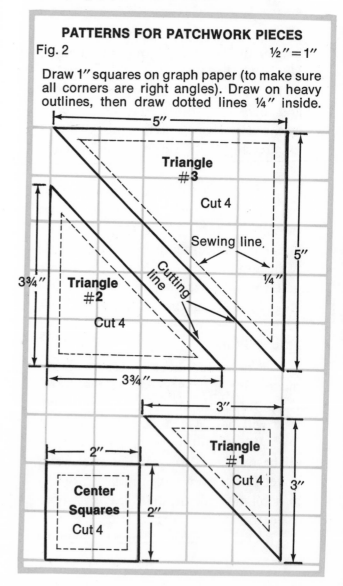

PATTERNS FOR PATCHWORK PIECES

Fig. 2

½" = 1"

Draw 1" squares on graph paper (to make sure all corners are right angles). Draw on heavy outlines, then draw dotted lines ¼" inside.

5"

Triangle #3 — Cut 4

Sewing line

Cutting line

5"

¼"

3¾" — Triangle #2 — Cut 4

3¾"

3" — Triangle #1 — Cut 4

3"

2"

Center Squares — Cut 4

2"

If you have trouble finding the best spot on a patterned fabric, draw the small triangle on a piece of scrap paper. Cut out, making a triangular hole (Fig. 3). Lay this over the design on the fabric, moving it around until the best part of the design shows. Remove, place pattern in this spot. Repeat for other size pieces.

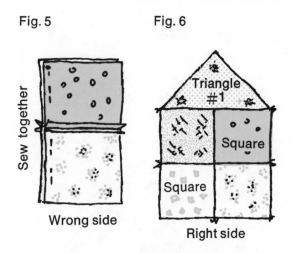

Fig. 5

Fig. 6

Sew together

Wrong side

Triangle #1

Square

Square

Right side

Fig. 3

Fig. 4

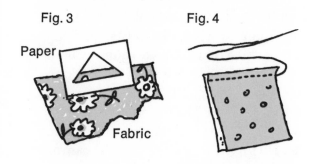

Paper

Fabric

After planning fabric and colors for each shape, pin patterns on fabric and cut out each shape. For each patched square, four pieces of each shape will be needed (sixteen pieces in all).

Pin two squares together, right sides of material facing each other. Using tiny running stitches (Fig. 4), sew together sides of two squares, making ¼″ seams. Then sew the other two squares. Press open seams. Now pin together the two sewn units (Fig. 5) forming the center square of the patch. Always make sure right sides are together so seams will be on the wrong side. Make sure corners meet exactly in center. Sew together.

Sew long side of triangle #1 to edge of patched piece (Fig. 6). Repeat on all sides and press flat.

Pin long side of triangle #2 to edge of sewn piece. Make sure corner of center square hits exactly at center of triangle piece so the point is complete. Sew and repeat on other sides (Fig. 7).

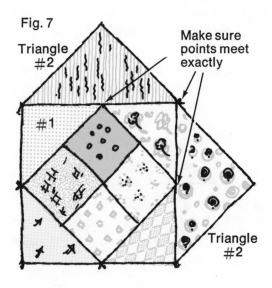

Fig. 7

Triangle #2

Make sure points meet exactly

#1

Triangle #2

41

Pin long side of triangle #3 to sewn piece, making sure each triangle is complete and the points hit properly. Sew. Pin on other sides; sew. One square is now completed (Fig. 8).

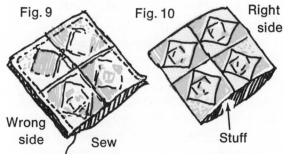

Fig. 9

Wrong side

Sew

Fig. 10

Right side

Stuff

Fig. 8

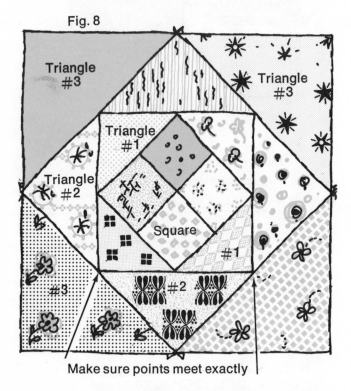

Triangle #3

Triangle #3

Triangle #1

Triangle #2

Square #1

#1

#2

#3

Make sure points meet exactly

Make four of these squares. Sew together, and it is big enough for a pillow. For the pillow back, cut fabric piece the size of the completed four-square unit. Place right sides together, and sew ¼″ seam (by machine if possible) around outside edge of three sides (Fig. 9). Turn right side out, press. Stuff (Fig. 10). To complete pillow, fold in ¼″ each edge of open side and sew together (see page 8).

For quilts: make six squares for a doll's bed; twenty squares make a crib quilt. Piecework needs padding and backing to complete quilt. Cut a plain piece of fabric for backing about 2″ wider all around than the quilt. Fold and pin top and bottom of backing material around an old picture frame (Fig. 11) or an artist's canvas stretcher which is sold at art stores. Baste padding in position; then place piecework, right side up, over backing and padding (Fig. 12). Pin and baste the three layers together. Quilt a section at a time. When complete, remove from frame and take out all bastings. Cut under layers even with top (piecework), and sew a binding around all edges.

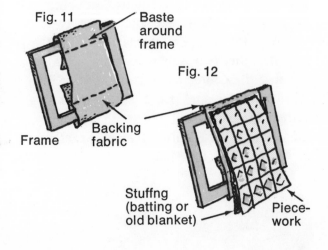

Fig. 11

Baste around frame

Fig. 12

Frame

Backing fabric

Stuffng (batting or old blanket)

Piecework

RUGS

Room showing design stenciled on a floor cloth

The homes of wealthy colonists had carpets imported from Europe or the Orient. But such floor coverings were just too expensive for most people. Instead, some homes had painted or stenciled designs on the wood flooring. Or the floor was often covered with a cloth made of a heavy canvas similar to that used for sails of ships. These floor cloths were given several coats of paint, and designs were added by the home-owner or the local painter.

When rugs were used, they were made of old scraps of precious fabrics.

These rag rugs were made in various ways. Weaving fabric strips through heavy warp thread was one method. Or folded cloth strips could be braided and sewn together. To make a hooked rug, yarn or narrow strips of fabric were pulled up about ¼″ through a coarse backing with a hook. Still another method used was to sew strips of fabric into a folded form which were then sewn to a backing. Braided corn husks made good mats for use at the entrance of homes.

Miniature Braided Rug

Materials Needed: About four pairs of discarded nylon stockings or panty-hose, household dye, a needle, thread and scissors.

Shades of natural tans are good for most of the rug, but use lighter and darker colors also. Dye some stockings brown, orange, or green. Or use colored stockings or pantyhose, if available. One pair of very dark brown or black stockings or pantyhose will be needed for the border.

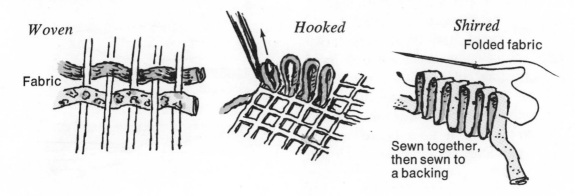

Woven

Fabric

Hooked

Shirred

Folded fabric

Sewn together, then sewn to a backing

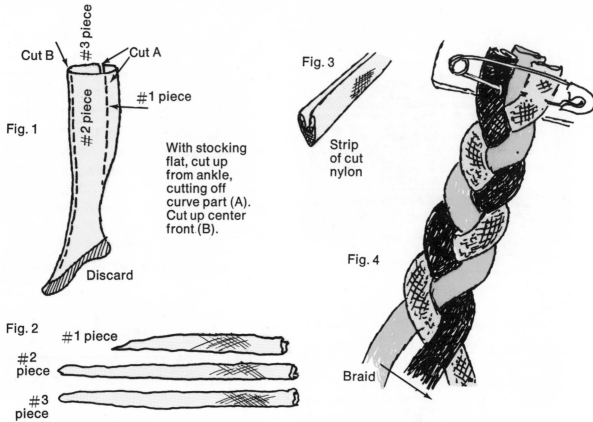

Fig. 1

#3 piece

Cut B

Cut A

#1 piece

#2 piece

With stocking
flat, cut up
from ankle,
cutting off
curve part (A).
Cut up center
front (B).

Discard

Fig. 2

#1 piece

#2
piece

#3
piece

Fig. 3

Strip
of cut
nylon

Fig. 4

Braid

Cut off the heavier parts of the stocking (tops and toes) and throw away. Lay stocking flat and cut as shown (Fig. 1, A and B). This makes three strips (Fig. 2) from each stocking leg (one strip is shorter). Cut all the stockings in this way.

Pull the strips gently and they will roll, keeping edges inside (Fig. 3).

To braid, use three strips: two strips of one color, and another strip of a contrasting color. With a big safety pin, pin together two long strips and one short. Then pin this onto a old cushion or clip it to a board with a clothespin. Start braiding: left side over,

right side over left, and so on (Fig. 4). Braid tightly, keeping braid flat. Don't let it twist.

When short strip ends, sew on another strip (Fig. 5, A and B), using color desired. Continue to braid and sew on new strips as needed. To keep a comfortable working distance, move up braided part and re-pin.

Fig. 5

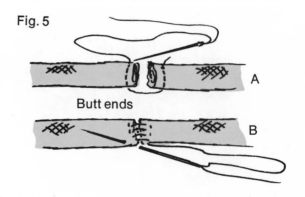

Butt ends

A

B

Use up all the cut strips, making various combinations of colors. Or sometimes braid three in strips of the same color.

Now the braid is ready to sew into a rug. Remove pin and lay the braid on a table. Coil the braid around, keeping it flat on the table. With needle and thread, sew braid from center out to next row (Fig. 6). Continue sewing loosely between inner braid and each added-on row around (Fig. 7).

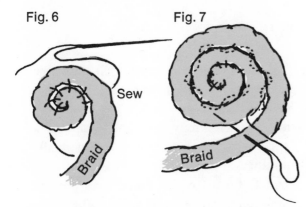

Fig. 6   Fig. 7

Sew

Braid

Braid

Keep work flat. If rug becomes cone-shaped, braid is being pulled too tightly. As you sew braid to inner braid, ease it in (Fig. 8). If rug tends to ruffle, too much outer braid is being gathered to previous row. Pull on outer row slightly as you sew it. (Fig. 9).

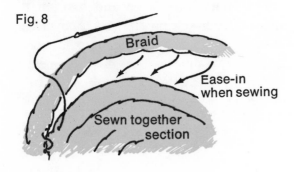

Fig. 8

Braid

Ease-in when sewing

Sewn together section

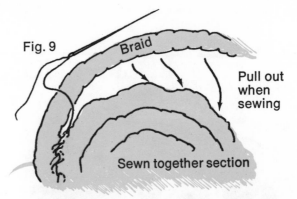

Fig. 9   Braid

Pull out when sewing

Sewn together section

When you have sewn together almost enough braid for the rug, unbraid the last 1″. Cut ends, making strips narrower (Fig. 10). Re-braid and sew to edge.

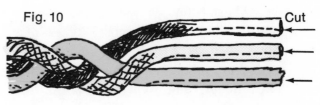

Fig. 10   Cut

For edging, braid a strip that is dark brown or black. You will need it long enough to fit all the way around the rug. Sew onto rug. Butt ends and sew together (Fig. 11). Press rug flat either with a steam iron or with a damp rag over rug. Place in the model room.

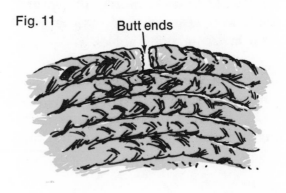

Fig. 11   Butt ends

RECREATION AND TOYS

Up at dawn with endless chores to be done, did colonial children ever have any fun? They certainly did.

When the chores were done, young children played many types of games such as racing, tag, and blind man's buff. They flew homemade kites, rolled hoops, and went swimming. In the North, there was sleigh riding and ice skating in the winter.

The children also enjoyed playing with toys. Nearly all toys were homemade, usually of wood. There were wooden dolls, toy soldiers, rocking horses, tops and alphabet blocks. Children often whittled their own wooden whistles and made cornstalks into make-believe swords or spears. Dolls were also made of rags, flowers, corn husks, or dried apples.

Pastimes which we think of as recreation were often essential for the colonists. Nothing was done just to "pass time". Fathers and sons went hunting and fishing—but not for fun. They were getting the family's food supply. Women worked while socializing at "husking bees," where corn was prepared for the winter, or at "quilting bees," where a quilt was completed. The average colonial family found their enjoyment in friendly gatherings and most everyone actively took part in games and recreation; few were satisfied watching activities.

Whirligig

A variety of toys with movable parts which flipped, turned, or twirled were whittled of wood. One such toy, the whirligig, may have been set on a fence post or held by a child while running. Each figure had exaggerated large flat arms which could spin around when they caught the wind. The head and body were generally carved out of one piece of wood and the arms were added on. An easier way to make a whirligig is to assemble it from several available pieces.

Materials Needed: One wooden drapery rod end, one large and two small spools (from sewing thread), one piece of wood 1″ thick (see Fig. 1 for dimensions), two pieces of ¾″ diameter dowel (5½″ long), one piece 3/16″ dowel (6¼″ long), two wooden paint stirrers, two large-holed beads (or wash-

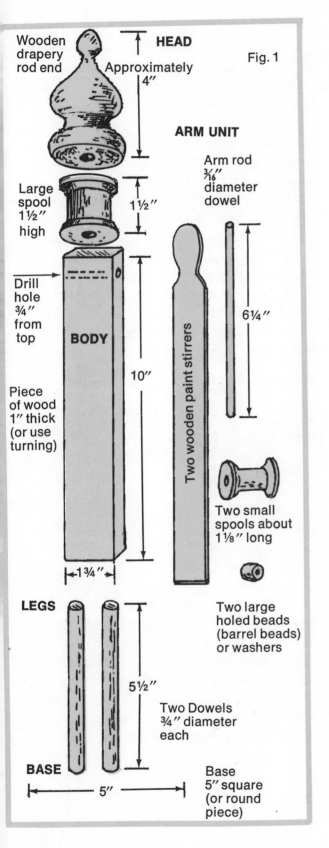

Fig. 1

Wooden drapery rod end

HEAD

Approximately 4″

ARM UNIT

Arm rod ³⁄₁₆″ diameter dowel

Large spool 1½″ high

1½″

Drill hole ¾″ from top

BODY

Two wooden paint stirrers

6¼″

10″

Piece of wood 1″ thick (or use turning)

1¾″

LEGS

Two small spools about 1⅛″ long

Two large holed beads (barrel beads) or washers

5½″

Two Dowels ¾″ diameter each

BASE

5″

Base 5″ square (or round piece)

ers). For base, use a 5″ square of ¾″ thick wood, or any wooden object of suitable size such as one side of a hamburger press, an old wooden salad bowl (inverted), or a large coaster.

Also needed are wood glue, two nails, toothpicks, paste wax, base paint or primer (white latex), colored acrylic or enamel paints (blue, white, black, and brown), gold-headed thumbtacks, dark brown furniture stain, and a 12″ piece of gold cord (the kind usually sold for gift wrapping). Tools needed are a small saw, knife, hand drill, awl, and hammer.

[Instead of using body shown, you may want to design your own. Most any combination of wooden shapes can make an interesting figure. In a lumber yard, ask for a turning about 12″ long or for a spindle post, which is used for assembling bookshelves (see Fig. 2). Or stack spools to height your design calls for].

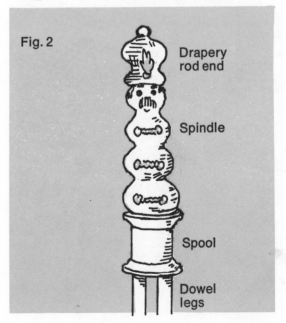

Fig. 2

Drapery rod end

Spindle

Spool

Dowel legs

To insert arm rod, drill a hole through the body piece at shoulder level (Fig. 1). Make sure arm rod (3/16″ dowel, 6¼″ long) slides through; it must turn easily in this hole.

Glue all body pieces together. Hammer two nails up through the base, about 1¼″ apart, into ends of leg dowels. Add glue and affix legs to base. Glue body to legs.

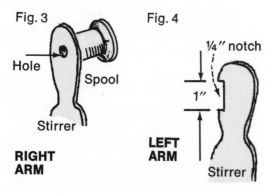

Fig. 3

Hole

Spool

Stirrer

RIGHT ARM

Fig. 4

¼″ notch

1″

LEFT ARM

Stirrer

For right arm, drill hole in stirrer to match hole in spool (Fig. 3).

For left arm, saw a ¼″ notch in the other stirrer about 1″ long to fit over end of spool (Fig. 4). Slide spool onto rod and glue stirrer to spool and rod (Fig. 5). Break a few pieces of toothpicks, add glue, and

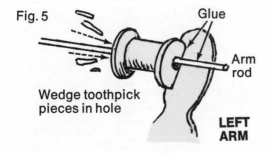

Fig. 5

Glue

Arm rod

Wedge toothpick pieces in hole

LEFT ARM

wedge pieces into hole at other end of spool. It is *very important* that this spool be firmly attached to the stick. Allow to dry.

Rub a little wax onto arm rod in area that will be between the spools so it will turn smoothly. Slide on one bead (or washer); slide rod through hole in body, add other bead (or washer) on other side. Slide right arm spool onto arm rod. Insert and glue toothpick pieces inside right arm spool so spool will not turn on rod. Make sure beads do not touch the body (Fig. 6). Leave about ⅛″ on each side of body. Rod should turn freely in body.

Fig. 6

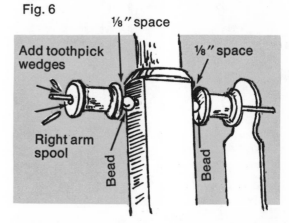

⅛″ space

Add toothpick wedges

⅛″ space

Right arm spool

Bead

Bead

Glue right arm stirrer stick to end of spool making one arm up and one down as shown in Fig. 7. Like a windmill, this position makes the whirligig catch the wind better and keep turning.

Allow glue to dry. Check to be sure both spools are firm on the rod; if not, add more glue and more toothpick wedges.

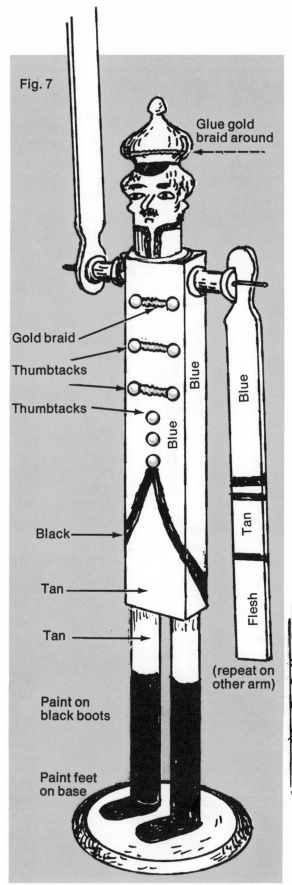

Fig. 7

Glue gold braid around

Gold braid

Thumbtacks

Thumbtacks

Blue

Blue

Blue

Blue

Tan

Flesh

(repeat on other arm)

Black

Tan

Tan

Paint on black boots

Paint feet on base

Give entire figure a base coat of white latex paint. Let dry and then paint with colors, making any kind of character you want: soldier (Fig. 7), or a policeman or an official in fancy clothes—all popular characters for colonial whirligigs.

For a soldier, paint black boots with feet painted right onto the base (Fig. 7). Paint jacket and hat blue. Mix colors to make tan (or white) trousers, brown hair, skin color for face and hands. With a fine brush, paint features in black (Fig. 8).

Glue 1″ pieces of gold cord on chest as shown in Fig. 7. Glue a piece of gold cord around hat. For buttons, use an awl to make holes in places shown in Fig. 7. Add glue to tips of gold-headed thumbtacks and push in place. Also add two thumbtacks in back. (Fig. 9).

To give it an old antiqued look, brush brown furniture stain over entire figure. Wipe off immediately.

Fig. 8

FEATURES
(actual size)
Trace if necessary

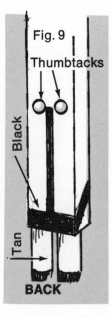

Fig. 9

Thumbtacks

Black

Tan

BACK

49

Dolls

Parents often made dolls for their children using every kind of available material. Father carved dolls of wood, sometimes attaching legs and arms with pegs so they could move. Other dolls with wooden heads and shoulders had stuffed leather bodies. As fabrics became more plentiful, rag dolls were made in every size and shape from scraps. Dolls with stuffed bodies sometimes had a head made from a gourd, nut, or dried apple. Stuffing was grass, straw, pine needles, or sawdust.

Children of the wealthy families often had dolls imported from Europe. These exquisite dolls had heads of wax, porcelain, or china and were dressed in silk clothing. By the eighteenth century, European factories made puppet and dolls' heads of papier-mâché. These too were imported by the colonists. All dolls looked like adults. There were no "baby" or child-shaped dolls.

Stuffed Doll:

Materials Needed: To make this 15″ doll, you will need papier-mâché (Celluclay), three 12″ pipe cleaners, a 1¼″ diameter ball of Styrofoam brand plastic foam and a small ½″ thick piece of Styrofoam, and a piece of tan or brown sturdy medium-weight cotton fabric (such as percale) for the body. Thread, needle, some brown or tan yarn, Sobo glue, black and a skin color paint (acrylic is good), fine sandpaper, serrated knife and some type of stuffing such as cotton or Dacron will also be needed.

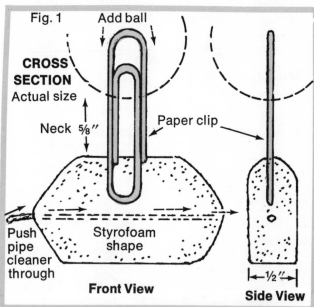

Fig. 1
Add ball

CROSS SECTION
Actual size

Neck 5/8″

Paper clip

Push pipe cleaner through

Styrofoam shape

Front View

├─½″─┤

Side View

To make head and shoulders, cut the ½″ Styrofoam into a piece about 2½″ x 1⅛″. Cut and taper edges to make shape shown in Fig. 1. This is actual size. Push one of the pipe cleaners through the middle of the Styrofoam (to attach arms later). For neck, push a

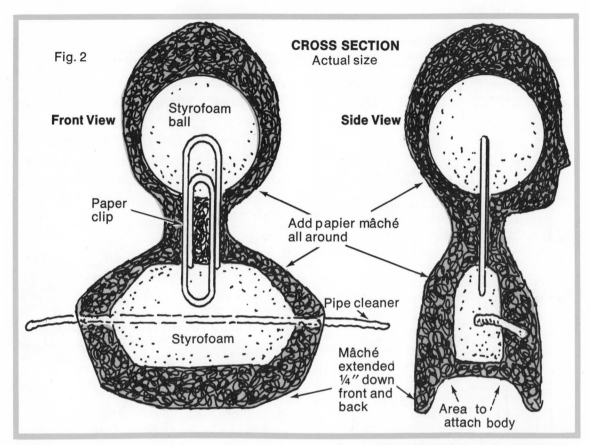

Fig. 2

CROSS SECTION
Actual size

Front View

Styrofoam ball

Paper clip

Add papier mâché all around

Side View

Pipe cleaner

Styrofoam

Mâché extended ¼″ down front and back

Area to attach body

large-sized paper clip down into center of shoulder piece (Fig. 1) and push ball on other end of paper clip. Or use a stick 1½″ long for neck.

Mix the papier-mâché, following directions on Celluclay package. Put a small amount of dry ingredients in a bowl—add about same amount of water. Mix and add more water if necessary to make mâché that will shape easily. Keep a bowl of clean water on hand, and dip your fingers in if they get sticky. Wet fingers also help make the papier-mâché thinner when needed to blend it better into the Styrofoam. Cover the ball and shoulder piece with papier-mâché, blending into Styrofoam. Shape neck,

chin, and head, and nose. Look at Fig. 2 which is actual size. Compare your shape, the front and the side, in order to get proper contours. Below shoulders, extend papier-mâché down about ¼″, front and back (see Fig. 2, side view), creating an area to attach body (see also Fig. 6). Allow to dry. Shape the doll's hands of papier-mâché, or carve them of ¼″ balsa wood, using pattern (Fig. 3).

When the papier-mâché is thoroughly dry, use sand paper to smooth

Fig. 3

ARM PATTERN (actual size)

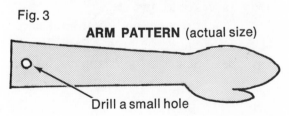

Drill a small hole

51

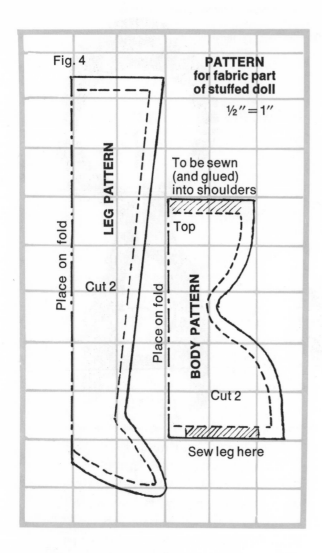

Fig. 4

PATTERN for fabric part of stuffed doll

½″ = 1″

LEG PATTERN

Place on fold

Cut 2

To be sewn (and glued) into shoulders

Top

BODY PATTERN

Place on fold

Cut 2

Sew leg here

the body (Fig. 5). Turn pieces right side out and stuff. Pin lower edge of body closed temporarly to hold stuffing in.

To attach body, add Sobo glue to underside of papier-mâché piece and to top of stuffed body piece. Push stuffed piece firmly up into area formed at base

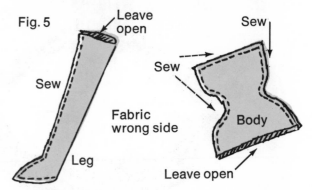

Fig. 5

Leave open

Sew

Sew

Sew

Fabric wrong side

Leg

Body

Leave open

of papier-mâché piece (Fig. 6). Chest and back should come over fabric about ¼″. Allow glue to dry thoroughly.

For legs, fold top edges flat, placing seam in center front, baste. Sew top of leg to lower edge of back of body (Fig. 7). Lay doll flat, legs in normal position. Fold under ¼″ front lower edge of body piece and sew to back with legs between (Fig. 8). To reinforce joinings at edges of legs, add extra stitches as you sew.

face and hands. Paint surfaces a skin color.

Enlarge body and leg patterns (Fig. 4). Draw patterns on a folded piece of paper. Trace other side, and open up for complete pattern. Cut two body pieces and two legs.

Sew up side and bottom seams of each leg along the dotted lines. Leave top open. Sew side and top seams of

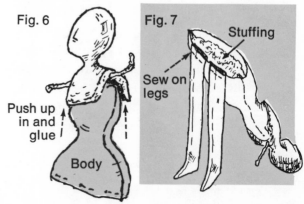

Fig. 6

Push up in and glue

Body

Fig. 7

Stuffing

Sew on legs

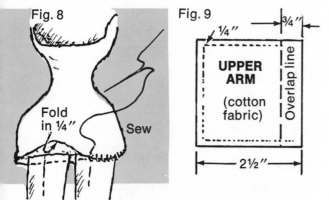

Fig. 8

Fold
in ¼″

Sew

Fig. 9

¾″

¼″

UPPER ARM (cotton fabric)

Overlap line

2½″

For arms, cut two 2½″ square pieces of cotton fabric. Mark ¾″ overlap (Fig. 9). Turn under ¼″ and baste three sides.

Twist pipe cleaners protruding at each shoulder to make loops on each side. Using another pipe cleaner, put one end through shoulder loop (Fig. 10), and bend down and twist end. Slide other end of this pipe cleaner through hole in hand piece and bend up, twist closed. Arm, from shoulder to finger tip, should be about 5½″ long.

Bunch some stuffing around the exposed pipe cleaner and lay one fabric piece around (Fig. 11). It should go around and overlap. If not, add or remove stuffing as needed. Judge for yourself when arm is proper thickness. Pin

overlap and sew edges. To keep stuffing in, sew ends closed around pipe cleaners at shoulder and against wood or papier-mâché at other end (Fig. 12). Repeat for other arm.

Tie

Fig. 13

Trim

Fig. 14

Make hair of yarn, fake hair, or string. Cut strands about 10″ long, and tie together in middle. Add glue to top and back of head; glue on hair (Fig. 13). Arrange and gather hair at back of neck and tie with a narrow ribbon or string (Fig. 14). Trim, so ends hang about 1¼″ below bow. Use black paint and a small brush to paint on eyes and mouth. Trace Fig. 15, if necessary, for placement of features.

On page 55, instructions are given to make a colonial dress and cap to complete a reproduction of an old doll.

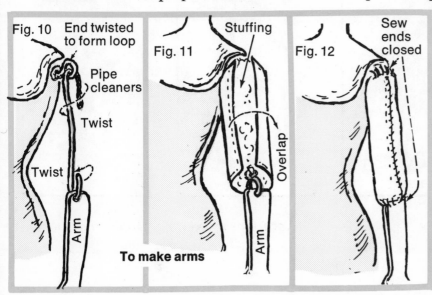

Fig. 10 End twisted to form loop

Pipe cleaners

Twist

Twist

Arm

Fig. 11 Stuffing

Overlap

Arm

Fig. 12 Sew ends closed

To make arms

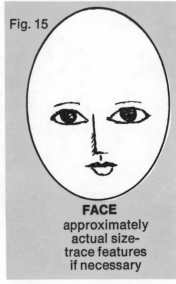

Fig. 15

FACE
approximately
actual size-
trace features
if necessary

CLOTHING

Wealthy people of the colonies followed fashions and style changes from Europe. Clothing was often made of silk and brocade. The men wore knee breeches and waistcoats covered with buttons and frills. The women wore wide skirts which stood out from the hips. At times, the skirt was slit in front and pulled back to show petticoats which were often quilted or embroidered.

Fashion dolls, brought from Europe, were dressed in the latest styles to help people copy new fashions. The rich had a dressmaker or tailor make their clothing, using these dolls for style since there were no patterns.

The average people wore more practical clothes made of sturdy, durable fabrics. Women wore dresses with a tightly laced bodice, long skirts covered with an apron and usually some sort of a cap covered the head. Men wore loose shirts. Their pants generally came just below the knee. Everyone wore shoes with large buckles of brass or pewter.

Children, up to the age of four or five, wore loose garments. By six, they wore the same style clothing as the adults.

High style clothes
(worn by the wealthy)

Everyday clothes
(worn by the working people and poor)

Doll's Dress

Sketch of a doll from the late 1700's

Make the doll first. Instructions start on page 50. You could make this dress for a 14″ to 16″ high-fashion type doll, but the patterns might have to be adjusted to fit your doll.

Materials Needed: For dress, ⅓ yard fabric; for cap and apron, 9″ x 12″ piece white cotton fabric; for sleeve trim, 8″ of white lace or eyelet edging ½″ or ¾″ wide; sewing thread to match fabric; a 20″ piece of white double-fold bias binding; ¾ yard elastic cord; ⅓ yard ¼″ wide trimming (floral ribbon or trim that looks like a row of flowers); two small snap fasteners. Also

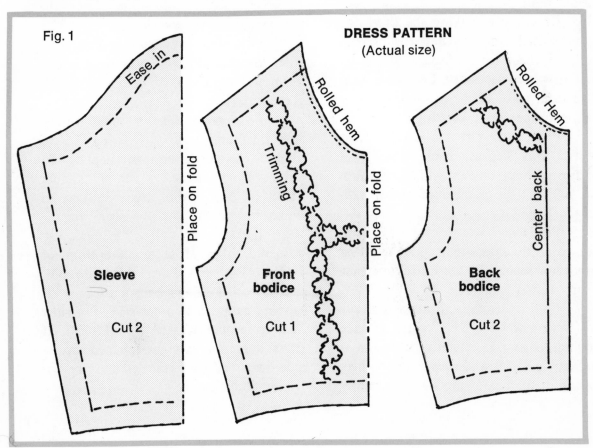

Fig. 1

DRESS PATTERN
(Actual size)

Ease in

Place on fold

Sleeve

Cut 2

Rolled hem

Trimming

Place on fold

Front bodice

Cut 1

Rolled Hem

Center back

Back bodice

Cut 2

needed are pins, paper for patterns, one needle with a large enough hole to sew with the elastic cord, and a regular sewing needle.

For dress, any color fabric is fine. Use a scrap if a large enough piece is available. Cotton is suggested, but doll's clothes, especially on imported dolls, were often of fine fabric such as silk. A fabric with a small print design could be used. Make all seams ¼".

On folded paper, trace the sleeve and front bodice (Fig. 1). Trace other side, and open up for complete pattern. Trace back bodice pattern (Fig. 1). For skirt, cut a piece 24" wide and 10½" long.

[If you are making the dress for a purchased doll, lay patterns around doll and check for proper size. Re-draw pattern where necessary. For skirt, measure from waist to toe tip and add ¾" to get proper skirt length.]

First, cut skirt out of the dress fabric. Pin sleeves, back, and front bodice patterns on remaining dress fabric, and cut the number of pieces indicated (Fig. 1).

Pin two back bodices to front bodice at shoulder—right sides together —and sew seams. To finish neckline, sew a tiny rolled hem (Fig. 2).

Fold under the end of each sleeve ⅛" and sew on a 2½" piece of lace edging, easing in slightly to make a ruffle (Fig. 3). Sew sleeves to the bodice, easing in fullness at top so it fits neatly

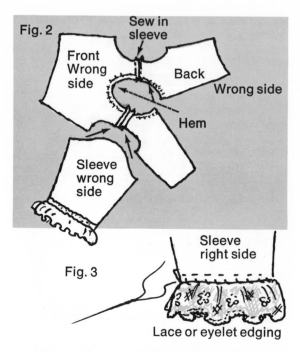

Fig. 2 — Sew in sleeve — Front Wrong side — Back — Wrong side — Hem — Sleeve wrong side

Fig. 3 — Sleeve right side — Lace or eyelet edging

into the armhole (see Fig. 2).

Fold front over back bodice, right sides together (Fig. 4). Sew right sleeve seam and right side of bodice (Fig. 4). Repeat on left side.

Fold skirt piece in half, wrong side out, and sew ¼" seam. Leave about 2" from top unsewn (Fig. 5). To gather skirt, make a running stitch about ¼" from top edge. Pull up to make top about 4½" around (or fit waist measure of doll). Pin and sew gathered edge of skirt to bottom of bodice (Fig. 6). Turn right-side out, and try on doll. Pin back closed, overlapping as much as necessary. Pin skirt hem to proper length (tip of toes). If dress does not fit right, put on wrong side out, adjust seams, and re-sew where necessary.

Fig. 4

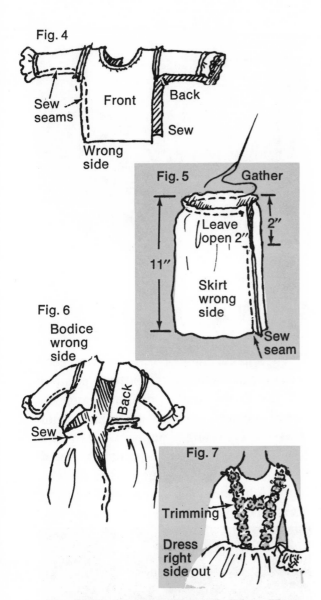

Fig. 5

Fig. 6

Fig. 7

Fig. 8

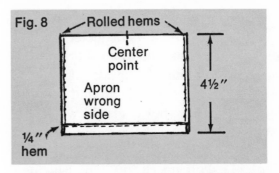

For apron, cut piece of white fabric 5½″ x 4½″. Hem as shown (Fig. 8). Place a pin to mark top center point. Gather unfinished edge to 2″. Mark centerpoint on the 20″ piece of bias binding. Pin center points together and sew gathered piece to one edge of binding (Fig. 9). Fold binding over other side of apron and pin. Fold and pin together tape edges on each side of gathered piece. Sew tape closed (Fig. 10), and continue sewing over gathered piece, making ties and completing apron.

Hem bottom edge of skirt. Hem each edge of back opening, allowing for overlap. Sew on tiny snaps for closing (or sew back closed later when completed, if doll is for display only). Place dress on doll again and pin floral trimming as shown (Fig. 7). Remove dress, and sew on trimming.

Fig. 9

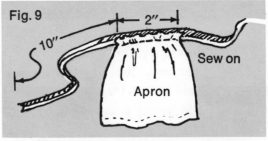

Fig. 10

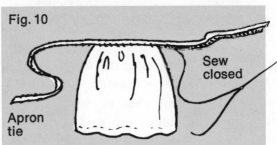

For cap, use a 6″ diameter saucer and draw a circle on white fabric. Cut out. Mark a line ¾″ inside of circle. Make a rolled hem all around circle. Thread the large-holed needle with the elastic cord, and make a running stitch along marked line, gathering up fabric (Fig. 11). Pull up elastic until cap fits snugly on doll's head. Tie the elastic in a knot and cut off, leaving ½″ ends. Adjust on the head so it puffs up properly (Fig. 12).

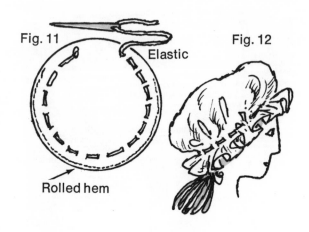

ARTS AND DECORATIVE CRAFTS

Early colonial homes tended to be a drab brown color. The fireplace was made of dark brick, and the walls and floor of dark pine wood. Wherever possible, color was added in the form of bright quilts, decorative plates, and hanging herbs. Through the winter, bouquets of dried flowers and grasses filled containers. By the middle of the eighteenth century, the fireplace wall in most homes was paneled, moldings added, and the room painted.

Wealthy families had elegant, attractive homes since they could afford imported porcelain, oil paintings, rooms papered with imported Chinese wallpaper, woodwork of rare woods, and Oriental rugs on the floor. The common folk wanted some of these things in their own homes, and they did whatever they could to imitate them.

Smaller homes often were decorated with designs or textures painted on the floors, walls, furniture, and on small objects such as containers and trays. Traveling painters carrying brushes and powdered paints, traveled from town to town. They often did the important painting and decorating, such as stenciling a wall to imitate wallpaper.

Room with a stenciled wall

Young ladies of fashionable families went to special schools to learn decorative arts such as embroidery, rolled paper work, painting on glass, wax working, and many others. Idle hands were considered sinful for anyone; even daughters of the wealthy were expected to keep themselves occupied at *all* times.

By 1750, although an average family still had many tasks, there was some free time. For brief moments family members might be more pleasantly occupied creating a decorative object for their home.

Boxes covered with wallpaper or cut out pictures (decoupage)

Cut paper design (Paper Lace)

Cut paper portrait (Silhouette)

Paper

In colonial times little or no paper was ever thrown away. Not only was it made by hand, but rags which were used were also scarce. Handmade paper was thick and durable. It was pricked, pressed, cut, painted, or curled for various decorative effects.

By folding a piece of paper once or twice and cutting away small areas, designs were formed. In skilled hands, this simple process resulted in delicate paper lace shapes.

Some people were talented at cutting small portraits out of paper. These were painted black and framed.

Wallpaper was imported and expensive. Any leftover pieces were used, often to cover or line boxes. Designs were cut out and glued onto objects for decoration. Decoupage, popular in France, was also done in the colonies. In this process, small cut-out pictures were glued in an arrangement onto a wood surface, then covered with many layers of varnish.

Potichomania:

Potichomania, another kind of picture pasting, was created to imitate the lovely and expensive imported Chinese vases. To make a vase, select a

Fig. 1

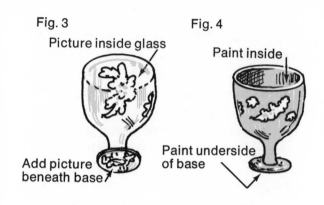

Fig. 3
Picture inside glass
Add picture beneath base

Fig. 4
Paint inside
Paint underside of base

glass such as a brandy snifter or wide-mouthed jar (Fig. 1). Any glass or jar will do as long as its opening is big enough to get your fingers around inside. Wash the glass inside and out, and dry.

Look through magazines, wall-paper samples, mailing brochures, and old greeting cards for small pictures. Christmas card catalogs from museums have reproductions of famous pictures of a good size. These pictures will be glued to the inside of the glass, facing out. The paper should not be too heavy.

Select several shapes with interesting outlines, but not with delicate pieces sticking out (Fig. 2). Carefully cut out each shape. Decide first where each shape will go by holding it inside the glass. Cut as many shapes as needed. If your glass has a base, plan to also add designs below the base (Fig. 3) so they show through.

To attach, use white glue, thinned slightly with water. Thoroughly cover right side of cut-out picture with glue. Place the cut-out shape inside of glass in spot planned. Rub with finger or soft cloth to make sure it is completely glued to glass and there are no air bubbles. Glue in the rest of the pictures, sliding shapes around if necessary. Don't worry about extra glue on glass; it won't show when finished. Allow to dry.

Select a paint color for this potichomania that compliments the pictures pasted inside. White, light blue or pale green are good. For certain pictures, black or dark red paint can be dramatic. Any type of paint can be used, but acrylic works best.

Paint the *inside* of the glass right over the glued-on pictures. At times, while painting, hold glass near light to see that paint is covering evenly. If base is decorated, paint underside (Fig. 4). Give second coat of paint after first dries, if necessary, to get an even color. When finished, fill with dried or artificial flowers.

Fig. 2

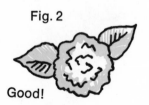

Good!

Not this
Use only the center flower

60

Pomander Ball

A quiet occupation for the children on a winter's night in the North was making pomander balls from the large supply of stored apples. In the South, oranges and limes were used, also. A pomander was an "air freshener", for the smells in a colonial home were not always pleasant. Pomanders were piled in bowls or set on shelves. Their fragrance was increased when held in the hand.

Materials Needed: To make a pomander ball, you must have a large apple, a box of cloves (from a supermarket), cinnamon, plastic net bag (onions are often packed in this type of bag) or 8″ square of nylon net (available in fabric stores), and cord, ribbon, or yarn.

Select a large firm apple such as MacIntosh or Golden Delicious. Prick the skin with a fork. Into each hole insert the stem of a whole clove (Fig. 1). Keep pricking and inserting cloves until the whole apple is completely covered. Place the apple in a shallow bowl and sprinkle with cinnamon. Set in a cool, dry spot for a few days. Then shake off any excess cinnamon.

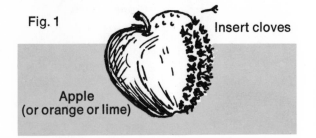

Fig. 1   Insert cloves

Apple
(or orange or lime)

To hang the ball, cut ends off a net bag making piece about 10″ long. Slip apple inside (Fig. 2). Gather ends at bottom; tie a bow with cord or bright-

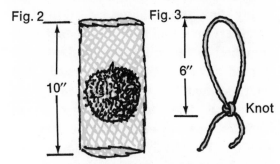

Fig. 2   10″   Fig. 3   6″   Knot

colored yarn. For hanging loop, cut 18″ piece of cord or yarn. Tie knot (Fig. 3), forming a 6″ loop. Gather net over top of ball, wind ends of cord around and tie another knot (Fig. 4). Tie a yarn bow over the knot and hang (Fig. 5).

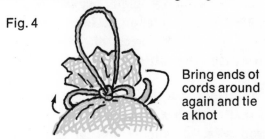

Fig. 4

Bring ends of cords around again and tie a knot

Or use an 8″ square of nylon net in attractive color. Place pomander ball in center, and gather net up around. Tie with cord (Fig. 6), making hanging loop as before. Hang up in the kitchen or other room.

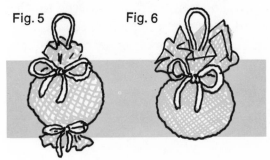

Fig. 5   Fig. 6

Wooden Eagle

Carving became a special art in the colonies because there were so many fine trees. Signs, store figures, weathervanes, and figureheads that were attached to the great sailing ships were carved of huge pieces of wood. The average man carved small pieces of wood into toys, household gadgets or whittled small wooden figurines for recreation. Practically every colonial boy owned a jacknife and had learned how to use it.

The eagle was one of the more popular subjects to be carved of wood. It officially became our national symbol in 1882. To get the feel of carving a three-dimensional shape, begin with this folded-wing eagle on a log. Carve it out of a single piece of balsa wood working from all sides.

Materials Needed: A block of balsa wood 6″ high x 3″ wide x 2″ deep, (if you want to practice by carving soap, get a large-sized double cake), coping saw, penknife (or pencil knife), sandpaper and brown stain.

Enlarge the patterns for the eagle on page 64 as indicated. (If using soap, make each pattern square only ¾″.)

To transfer the pattern to the wood, use carbon paper. Place side view on side of the block of wood with carbon paper between. Tape in place, trace outline, and then remove pattern (Fig.

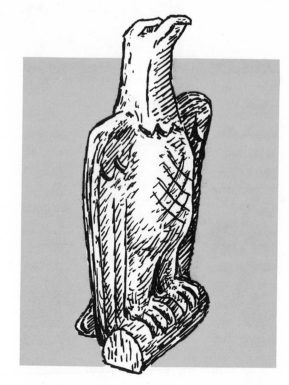

1). With coping saw, cut away excess wood, keeping at least ⅛″ away from drawn line.

With pencil, draw front view on the curved surface, marking width of neck and height of wings. Cut away excess (Fig. 2). Use back view as a guide for carving back of wings and tail.

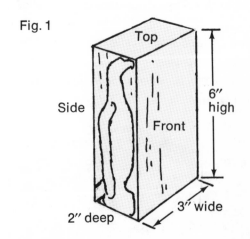

Fig. 1

Top

Side

Front

6″ high

3″ wide

2″ deep

Now you begin to whittle. With knife, cut off small pieces at a time to form the shape. With patterns as guides, round the head, point the beak, shape the body, cut wings back from body (Fig. 3). Make the feet around the log by cutting between claws (Fig. 4). Round back and shape tail (Fig. 5).

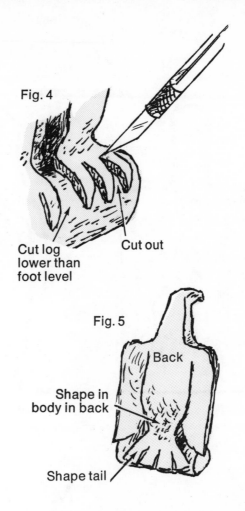

Fig. 4

Cut log lower than foot level

Cut out

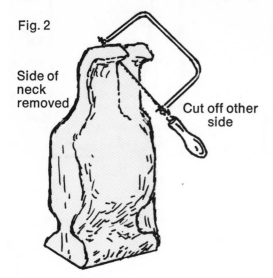

Fig. 2

Side of neck removed

Cut off other side

Fig. 5

Back

Shape in body in back

Shape tail

Make crossed lines (see pattern) on chest and back by cutting in ⅛″ grooves (Fig. 6 A and B).

Smooth and round the shape with fine sandpaper. To finish, stain a dark brown. (Liquid shoe polish also will give a nice brown color.)

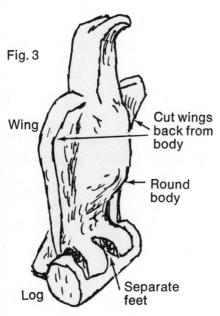

Fig. 3

Wing

Cut wings back from body

Round body

Log

Separate feet

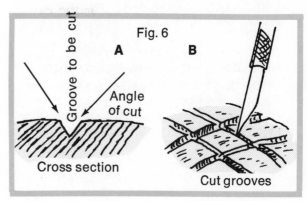

Fig. 6

Groove to be cut

A

B

Angle of cut

Cross section

Cut grooves

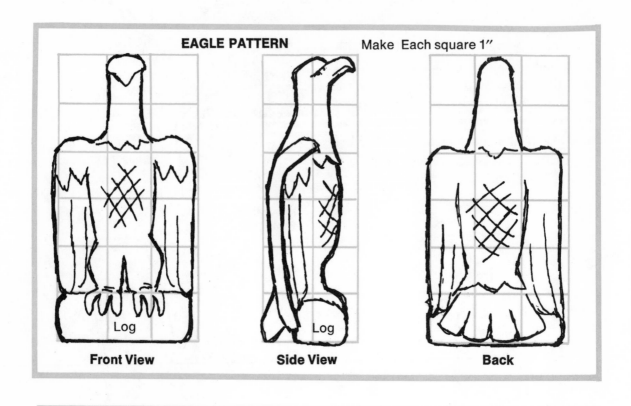

EAGLE PATTERN   Make Each square 1″

Log

Log

Front View   **Side View**   **Back**

MUSEUMS

Colonial crafts and folk art can be seen in many museums and historic restorations. Some have demonstrations of colonial crafts. Here is a brief list; there are many more. Be sure to write in advance.

THE BENNINGTON MUSEUM, Bennington, Vermont 05201

COLONIAL NATIONAL HISTORICAL PARK, P.O. Box 210, Yorktown, Virginia 23490

COLONIAL WILLIAMSBURG, INC. Goodwin Building, Williamsburg, Virginia 23185

COOPERSTOWN (FARMER'S MUSEUM), Cooperstown, New York

GREENFIELD VILLAGE AND HENRY FORD MUSEUM, Oakwood Blvd., Dearborn, Michigan 48121

N.Y. HISTORICAL SOCIETY, 170 Central Park W., New York, New York 10024

OLD MUSEUM VILLAGE OF SMITHS CLOVE, INC., Monroe, New York 10950

OLD STURBRIDGE VILLAGE, Sturbridge, Massachusetts 01566

PHILADELPHIA MUSEUM OF ART, Box 7646, Philadelphia, Pennsylvania 19101

SHELBURNE MUSEUM, Shelburne, Vermont 05482

THE SMITHSONIAN, 1000 Jefferson Drive SW., Washington, D.C. 20560

VAN COURTLAND MANOR RESTORATION, Croton-on-Hudson (write to: Sleepy Hollow Restorations, Inc., Tarrytown, N.Y. 10591)